MIKE PEY[

An Average War
Eighth Army to Red Army

Rookery Cottage, Rookery Lane, North Fambridge Chelmsford Essex CM3 6LP
Telephone and Fax: 01621 828545

Printed by Maypole Press & Publishing Company
South Woodham Ferrers, Essex CM3 5UW   Tel: 01245 32 31 30

Dedication
To those at the sharp end who ran out of luck

Acknowledgement:
Cover picture a carrier of the 4th Battalion Royal Northumberland Fusiliers

CHAPTER 1

When, in 1995, in the proverbial loft, I found a cardboard box full of letters I had written home during the war, I was stimulated by them to write my war down. An average sort of war, if you can call war average. Like thousands of others I worried that the war would be over before I got there so I gave the wrong age to get into the army. I fought in the Western Desert, was taken prisoner and, as such, was at first in Italy and then in Germany, from where after a couple of attempts I managed to escape and fight with the Russians until the war ended. As things were in those abnormal times - an average war.

I heard the declaration of war with Germany in a cyclists' tea shop near Southport. The motherly woman who ran the place could recognise what was once called "cannon fodder" when she saw it and was kindness itself. After all, it was only twenty one years since the Great War had finished and the tea shop was packed with young, fit, lively working class lads . . . what else could you call them? She knew a thing or two. Of the six names I can remember who listened to Chamberlain's speech on the wireless in that tea room on the 3rd of September 1939, Kirkman (we were in the same class at school) went down with the Prince of Wales when it was sunk off Malaya, Johnson after three years training with the Lancashire Fusiliers never got off the beach before he stopped a lump of shrapnel in his stomach on D Day, Hodnutt was wounded and patched up four times as he went through Europe with the East Lancashire Regiment, Ashford came home, as one would expect of RAF ground crew. My elder brother who was in minesweepers was also lucky and I too was one of the lucky ones. I think that was about par for the course. If you were at the sharp end approximately one in three would be unlucky. I have no doubt that the same scenario would have applied approximately to any half dozen lads in that tea shop.

It is difficult to believe now, but the day after the broadcast the recruiting offices were completely inundated and were turning volunteers away. I am sure, like me, those hopefuls didn't volunteer

Prewar, with my
older brother
(on the left).
The metal railings in
the background
disappeared to make
Spitfires.

entirely for King and Country and the realisation that Hitler had
to be stopped — he had already taken over Sudetenland, Austria
and Czechoslovakia and was now threatening Poland – but for the
chance of a bit of excitement. I doubt if any one of them had any
idea what war was. I know I hadn't. My father knew but couldn't
say anything to me about it as he also had volunteered for the last
war in 1914 just after being accepted for the police force. He
returned to go back down the mines with a limp, and was lucky to
still have two legs. In those days every adult knew what the war
had cost in the sacrifice of lives and were reminded about it every
year when everything, but everything, stopped at the eleventh
hour of the eleventh day of the eleventh month for the two
minutes' silence in memory of those who had been lost in the
1914-18 war. Armistice day and the wearing of a poppy was total
then and nationwide. My mother had lost her first husband. He
was one of five brothers all killed, three on the same day. In those
days one joined the local regiment, so losses tended to be localised

2

and concentrated. Pals' Battalions they were called. My uncle, an erstwhile regular, had left the mines to join the regular army and had travelled the Empire as a Sergeant in the Prince of Wales' bodyguard. When the war broke out, try as he might to get to France, he had been kept as an instructor at Fenham Barracks, the depot of the Northumberland Fusiliers, the regiment that I joined, a regiment that raised fifty three battalions. As an instructor he must have seen them all go off to France. Now with hindsight I realise what he must have thought. But not then.

I wasted a lot of time trying to get into the Navy. In those days it was the Senior Service and I assumed I would see the world. So it was for the Navy I volunteered. But when, at long last, I went for my medical I failed on the eyesight test. For the Senior Service you had to be physically A1 just like Hitlers SS.

Afterwards I realised it was all for the best. The snag that I later came to appreciate when the our battalion was being moved by the Navy was that in the Navy it was all or nothing – you could be standing on a mess deck travelling at a rate of knots and reading on the notice board what was on at some cinema in Alex the following week when – Wham! and you could be swimming. Nothing in the army was ever as sudden as that. A battalion survived. It may be battered, reduced – even decimated – but it was never final or instantaneous. You liked to think you were in with a chance and could do something about it. You might even be one of the L.O.B's (left out of battle) and so one of the nucleus of the battalion ready to be brought up to strength again.

I never considered the RAF, which needed about forty on the ground for every one that flew. And my eyesight and probably education, or lack of it, precluded flying. I realised later that the army fitted my way of thinking. It was all for the best. So as fate forced me to forgo the Navy I devoted my energies to the army recruiting offices.

While I was awaiting the results of my visits to these various recruiting offices I worked as a labourer in a print department of a rubber works. It was Jewish owned and now, thinking back on the conditions of work, I suppose it would be called a sweat shop.

The war quickly made itself felt and soon the print rollers were squeezing out camouflaged ground sheets. Some of the work we did had no camouflage printed on it and these, rumour had it, were for the dead. Conscription had become a fact of life and, as work mates got their calling up papers, farewell drinks in the local became common. Because we were now on war work some key workers became exempt from military service. Reserved occupation was for some the magic phrase and the owner's two sons and son-in-law started work at the factory and they were soon in this 'desirable' category.

The army had a far more visible presence in those pre-war days. Then Britain still had an Empire of sorts which needed troops, and many towns had barracks and the troops stationed there were a common sight. In those times, recruiting sergeants wearing a red sash were not an uncommon sight around the town. The tearaways and local lads who wanted a bit of excitement before settling down had always found a ready welcome in the local barracks. They later returned home tanned by Eastern suns and telling tales of the Sudan, Burma, and the North West frontier, so that the Recruiting Sergeant often was speaking to the converted. The snag with my local barracks was that I didn't want to join the Lancashire Fusiliers. Though living in Lancashire I was from the North and one of my family had always been in the Northumberland Fusiliers. Now it seemed the flow of conscripts was keeping them more than occupied without the need of volunteers. Nevertheless I kept visiting the Army recruiting offices.

In the meantime life went on and Radcliffe itself, where I lived, soon had its quota of troops. I think my mother would have liked me to be with them. One of the largest of the disused cotton mills had been taken over and converted into a huge office. It was manned by servicemen and women wearing the yellow flash of the Pay Corps. But what I wanted was the red flash of the Infantry.

Because of the town's proximity to Manchester and its docks we got a few bombs dropped in the area and because of these raids and the blackout the Saturday night visits to the Palais or skating rink took on a new excitement. Going into the light, warmth and movement of a dance hall from a totally blacked-out world stepped up the pleasure and contrast to an amazing degree. Uniforms were becoming common, though not as prevalent as they were to become later, when you would hardly see anyone in civvies at a dance hall. But these odd men out, the civilians, had some solid attractions – they would be in a reserved occupation and consequently earning good money, and they would be around for a long time. Going out from the light and warmth of these dances into total darkness was another pleasurable contrast especially if you had a feminine companion. The cameradie that existed in those days, or nights – because that is when most raids took place – was amazing but understandable. We were all in it together. Everyone had their blackout or bomb stories. One paper ran a regular cartoon titled 'Heard in the blackout' which was simply a totally black square with a caption underneath.

My bomb story happened when I was walking home one Saturday night during an air raid. There was all that went with an air raid, the ominous drone of the bombers overhead, the crump of bombs, the sound of the anti aircraft guns, the glow in the sky from fires and the sweeping searchlights. Always there would be the clamour of the bells of fire engines and ambulances and closer at hand the dangerous patter of razor sharp shell fragments hitting the road or the roofs and the voices of people as they watched, ready to dive into their shelters if something sounded as if it was going to come too close for comfort. I was passing along a street which was bordered by a park when a string of incendiary bombs (they were a little longer than a milk bottle) landed in the park. The recognised method of dealing with them was to use a stirrup pump. You stood on the base, put the suction end in a bucket of water and pumped out a spray of water onto the bomb through a short length of hose, spray being the operative word. All this string of bombs dropped harmlessly in the park except one, the last in the line, which landed sparking and spluttering on the road in front of the houses. In a matter of seconds it was surrounded by about a dozen enthusiastic people with buckets and stirrup pumps and all eager to put their training into practice. The spray started flying in no mean manner. The incendiary bomb was definitely outgunned and a voice from the darkness put these thoughts into words: "For Christ's sake give the little buggar a chance!"

The long walks home in the darkness from dances and skating rinks were now becoming common with trains and buses being put out of service or stopped by the raids but I never minded. I looked on them as training. The cycling club had faded away as the older and leading lights had been called up and I had started bog-trotting instead. Long walks over the moors now occupied my weekends. There are plenty of moors close at hand in Lancashire and most Sundays found me walking over some of them. Bogtrotting. Just as the cycling had been so pleasurable because there was so little traffic on the pre war roads the bogtrotting was possible because wherever you dropped down to on a Sunday night there would be a bus to get you home. Fewer people owned cars and for those that did petrol was rationed and then only to people who needed it for war work, consequently the bus services were necessary and good. A bonus was that the map and compass work needed to bring one down to some solitary pub on a moorland road where there would be a bus stop was to come in useful later.

On one of my Saturday nights out, the war was brought a little closer. Half of Europe had been over run before Britain declared war and for six or seven months after that nothing had happened. The Phoney War. Then came the Blitzkrieg. It was a new type of war – a war of movement. The German armoured columns raced across Europe and swept aside armies still trained and equipped to fight a static war in trenches. German paratroops created havoc with surprise attacks behind the Allied lines. They took fortresses by dropping on their roofs. The revolutionary Stuka diver bomber caused chaos miles behind the defenders. One by one like a row of dominoes the countries of Europe: Poland, Czechoslovakia, Holland, Austria, Belgium, Norway, Denmark and finally France fell to the German Panzers. The end result was the retreat from Dunkirk. As the troops that had been evacuated got back to England, they were simply crammed on trains and shipped off to garrison towns. I was in Bury town centre when a large group of them arrived at the station. They were soldiers but not soldiers, in uniform but dirty uniforms, some torn or with something missing, and many had additions such as civilian shoes, or a coloured pullover and very few had hats. But all had stories to tell. I can remember quite strongly that the overall reaction and feeling at that time, June 1940, was not of defeat, in fact just the opposite. Though every country in Europe had now been overrun the mood of the country was more of a feeling of relief, a sense of 'Well we know where we are now. We're on our own.' Churchill put it better – "their finest hour".

In 1940 my visits to the recruiting offices paid off and I got what I wanted. Merely getting into the services was easy, one just waited for one's call up, for conscription had been started in 1939. The snag was, like thousands of others, I didn't want to wait for my call up – I was impatient, the war might not wait for me. If you were under age they tried to make you join a young soldiers' battalion but if you did that you couldn't leave the country until you were an old man of twenty. I was pleading my case as I had done previously, at the recruiting office in Albert Square, Manchester, to no avail when the clerk – they were invariably old soldiers – asked me what regiment I wanted to join. I replied, "The Northumberlands". He considered, then said, "A good mob. They relieved us at Loos." I happily signed on the dotted line for what was termed Hostilities only.

When I got my call up papers to join the Northumberland Fusiliers at their depot in Newcastle on the 16th of October 1940 it was like going home. I had been born and brought up about eight miles away in the mining village of Houghton-le-Spring until my father had moved South to Lancashire to find work. All my relatives and childhood friends still lived there. I had often cycled back there for holidays, it was home ground.

The first day or two when I reported to Fenham barracks was a great disappointment. We weren't given a gun but had to sit down in a class room with paper and pencil to take aptitude tests. The end result was that our intake was divided into six platoons and I found myself in the top one. Because of this my first impression of army life was of a much more amenable standard than I had expected. The platoon I was now in was approximately fifty-fifty conscripts and volunteers and the majority of the other nineteen men in "A" Platoon with whom I now shared a hut had been educated at grammar schools or public schools. Some had come direct from University and one, the exception to the rule, was an ex corporal, a deserter from the Irish army. It stood out a mile. As Kipling put it:

"The sergeant arst no questions, but'e winked the other eye,

"E sez to me, 'Shun!' an' I shunted, the same as days gone by."

At that time England was a very class conscious society and accent was all. The right one signified education. Even the N.C.O.s who instructed us showed deference to those they knew would get commissions. For me it was a very interesting interlude. We were soon brain washed into the fact that the Royal Northumberland Fusiliers, (*motto Quo Fata Vocant, Where the Fates Call*) who were the Fifth of Foot and had fought in every battle worth fighting, was the finest regiment in the British Army, so consequently in the world, which is obviously correct. And that the Vickers machine gun was the finest weapon a soldier could have the good fortune to handle. I believed it then but later this had a negative effect, as I applied this thinking blanketwise to all machine guns, German and Italian included. We were also told that the Army could do anything to you except put you in the family way, I never had cause to doubt this. We were given our army number which went on every bit of kit we had. The last two numbers were added to everyone's name, for some such as myself Peyton 73 it was unneeded but for the Smiths and Jones they often got referred to by the numbers alone. That number was, is, still stamped indelibly on my memory. When later it was said of a bullet or a piece of shrapnel ' it had his number on it', it was that number they meant, his army number. Today the first four digits of my unforgettable army number were the obvious ones to use on my credit card. The other point which was drummed into us was that from now on everything in our life, every eventuality that could happen to a soldier and the correct procedure to take during and after that eventuality, was covered by King's Rules and Regulations.

The Platoon I was now in came under the care of an Irish Sergeant – he was later killed in Burma – who in his thick brogue told us that normally i.e. in peacetime, the machine gun course took two years, but due to extenuating circumstances, the war, this had of necessity been shortened to seven months. He made sure we did not waste any of this time.

After basic training on the rifle in which I did quite well, coming seventh in the company, our lives revolved around the Vickers gun. Morning, noon and night, breakfast, dinner and tea, we lived, ate, slept and dreamed machine guns. Even now, fifty years later, whenever I have to judge some weight I start with forty pounds and go up or down from there. This is because I can estimate forty pounds to the fraction of an ounce. Forty pounds was the weight of the tripod of a Vickers gun and I, we, carried them for miles. I say we carried them for miles with some truth as at that stage there were no trucks to carry them in. However the army got over that problem easily. In the exercises where we were supposed to have vehicles an oblong was chalked on the barrack square, not any old oblong but the exact area of a fifteen hundred-weight truck. After that had been drawn the operative phrase was 'going through the motions'. Into these chalked squares we went through the motions of loading and unloading our machine guns. Woe betide the man who stepped over the chalk mark before he had gone through the motions of unfastening and letting down the tailboard, or stepped over the line instead of going through the motions of jumping down. And in those early days if the guns had to go anywhere we carried them there and we carried them back. But our lessons went home. Even now I can still repeat parrot fashion, like prayers learnt as a child, the working principles of a Vickers machine gun: 'Upon the gun being fired the recoiling portions are forced to the rear by recoil assisted by gases which follow the bullet up the barrel and strike. etc.' We had one in the barrack room and often in the evening for our own satisfaction we would time each other stripping it down and reassembling it. Reading the letters now which I sent to my parents I wonder what they thought of them. They were eulogies on the machine gun, blow by blow accounts of training exercises. I have a letter starting, *'Yesterday we did a strategic withdrawal...'* and I related what I considered fascinating facts such as did they know that when the gun was being fired at two hundred rounds a minute there were always two ejected cartridge cases falling to the ground and yet the gun itself was only two foot six from the ground . . . ? We were motivated all right.

It may all have been part of the brain washing but 'A' Platoon, instead of fatigues in the cookhouse and such like, had to do telephone duty throughout the night. Telephones were not all that common in those days, few homes had them, so it was assumed that the members of 'A' platoon were intelligent enough to cope. It was a simple task, just sitting in the Company Office in case the phone rang. It seldom did, so you read. There was plenty of reading matter there, the Regimental Diaries, rows of them. They simply recorded in very factual down to earth language what long gone Fusiliers had done in the cause of duty. It was stirring stuff. I little thought that one day I would be detailed off to collect the information to bring them up to date.

A letter I wrote home at the time gives some idea of barrack life: *'At our break today I was looking out of the window overlooking the square and the youngsters from the married quarters had made a slide right across the square which has a slight incline on it and every soldier who had to cross the square made a detour so that he could slide down it, and they fairly kept the pot boiling. All the cars and trucks now have snow chains on and when they are slack they jingle just like bells, it sounds nice when there is a convoy going out. A red Post Office van got mixed up with one and it made me think of a tomato sandwich made with brown bread. Had a lesson today on tanks and how to stop them. It is marvellous how we remember all we are taught. In peace time it takes two years to make a proper machine gunner. We finish our training in four months besides learning driving, maintenance, the anti tank gun, Bren, the rifle, all war gases, signalling, fieldcraft, wiring, tactics, rifle drill and scores of other subjects and when you reckon there are 368 pieces in a Vickers alone and all the lot jumbled together can be put together by any lad in the squad and it will work afterwards, and we have to be almost as proficient with the other gun. It tickles you when you hear people say, "If he's dumb they'll have him in the army." I've done more sums, decimals, worked out more degrees and had more mental exercise in three months than in all the time I was in school. I think I have mentioned we have an adjutants' parade on Saturdays when all the companies are out with rifles cleaned, tin hats all at the same angle, boots polished, equipment spotless, heels clicking, sergeants shouting, butt slapping, band playing, drums rolling and last but not least the Regimental Sergeant Major shouting. I enjoy these parades except for the cleaning the night before. Well we've skipped it through the snow being on the ground and so instead of polishing my brass tonight I am polishing off this letter.'*

Throughout this period we unconsciously absorbed the ways of the army and I was taught to steal. A lot of my spare time was spent in the dance halls in Newcastle and at one of these dances my gas mask was stolen. Every one carried a gas mask in those days and they were left where ever was convenient in the dance hall. I returned and reported my loss to our corporal. He looked at me as if I was an idiot and told me to go and get myself another from where I had lost mine. For one not used to such methods it was quite a task, even in the semi darkness with hundreds to choose from. I grabbed one and scuttled out and back to barracks as if I had stolen the crown jewels. But the corporal wasn't satisfied. In the light of day it was obviously a very tatty and ancient one, so back I went. I wasn't as nervous this time, took it a bit more leisurely and picked up one that looked quite good. I was learning

– until it was opened up and we found it was a naval type with about a three foot breathing tube. The navy carried them on their hip, the army on its chest. Finally on my third attempt the Corporal declared himself satisfied. Even then I thought of the endless spiral I had set in motion. I had stolen three gas masks, that meant their three ex-owners would be now in the chain and doing the same and so ad infinitum.

During this time I was more fortunate than most of the others in that I had my relatives to go to whenever I had time off. It was an easy journey because in those days for anyone in uniform hitch hiking was the norm. We had to carry our gasmask at all times so I would go off with my gas mask case full of dirty washing and return with it full of cakes and pies. Obviously these were shared but with the appetites we had developed it was a bit like giving a donkey strawberries. I did have one exceptional meal about this time but I earned it. We had the company cross country run and our Platoon team, of which I was a member, won it. The Sergeant who beforehand had threatened us with all kinds of discomforts if we lost, said in front of the officer, "Just do your best bhoys and I'll be plaised". He was over the moon when we won. He and the twelve team-members sat at a flower bedecked table on a platform looking down on the dining hall and were waited on hand and foot. We ate and drank to our hearts' content as we re ran every stride of the race again. Two days later three of us were chosen to run for the Battalion. The ex-Irish corporal, who was considered a racing cert was one of them, and at the end of the race we found he did not like the British army any better than he had liked the Irish one. You could not leave the barracks in civilian clothes and obviously he had smuggled his out when going out in uniform and left them hidden in one of the patches of gorse on Fenham moor to be picked up later when not encumbered with an army uniform. i.e. when in running kit. Like many another racing cert he failed to finish. I finished in the first half, just, sixty ninth out of one hundred and forty.

Seven months after arriving in the barracks all of our platoon and most of the company passed out as proficient machine gunners and, except for those going to officer training units, moved into a holding company.

Life in a holding company was different. For one thing we left modern warm, well-built, insulated huts with showers and ample hot water to move into one of the large barrack blocks that surrounded the barrack square. The large barrack room we were now in had previously been hay lofts over stables, which had been saved from demolition by the 1914-18 war, then given a new lease of life by the war we were now involved in. It was as basic accommodation as one could get. It was about this time I thought it important enough to mention in a letter home that I had bought a book in a second hand shop. It was not a common practice for me. Although I read a lot, books were something that came from the local library and I cannot bring to mind a bookshop in Radcliffe at that time. The first book I bought and proudly owned was appropriate enough, Kipling's 'Barrack Room Ballads'. We were in these barracks during the winter and it was a hard one – in fact a lot of the holding company's time was spent in snow shifting. If there had been any air raids we would be on fatigues replacing the 4.5s shells, described in a letter so my mother could understand *"they are about four foot long and as round as a dinner plate at the bottom and are for the anti-aircraft guns."*

It was during an air raid that I heard a four handed conversation that stuck in my mind. The raid was going on and, all according to Standing Orders, we were in the trenches that had been dug for the purpose. In the trenches with us we had some Gordon Highlanders, who were another machine gun training Regiment. We were leaning on the top of the trenches looking at the glow in the sky against which were silhouetted the figures of two officers. We heard a very English voice remark, "Not many takers for the trenches tonight." The Gordon officer replied, "They'll be in the town spending their bawbees." There was a pause, then from somewhere in the darkness a Geordie voice asked, 'Hey Jock, hoo much is a bawbee warth?" There was a pause, then the reply, "About a farthing a ken." Another pause. "He's aboot reet then."

Our life still revolved around the Vickers gun and a letter home at the time telling of some tactical training exercise showed how the country as a whole was committed to the war . . . *'we had a day of tactics last week and landed cushy. We had a field phone rigged up and I was nursing it in a big house standing in its own grounds. Had a line leading from the lawn through the French windows into the library where I was sat in a little easy chair where the lady of the house brought me tea, biscuits and cigarettes if I needed them . She had three sons, one in the Army one in the Navy one in the Air Force and all with commissions. They must have been three good sports according to the books they had on the shelves, all travel books or sports like canoeing and such like. The daughter kept me company a bit, she had been out riding and came into the library to get something. I had noticed her taking her horse to the stable, for all their money they were not stand offish. It must have looked queer a large panelled library well stocked with books, polished floor, really thick carpets, a huge open fireplace and French windows leading onto the lawn where you could see the blokes on the chain of supplies passing up the ammunition to the gun pits and yours truly sat there in an arm chair with a cup of tea at my feet and a slice of cake and some biscuits on a plate beside it. On the other side my pencil note book and little field phone, cushy what. What more could I want – company, eats, drinks, a responsible job and books to browse in. It would not be so bad if I always get soft like that but the last time I was in a barn and the only eats was turnips they had stacked there for the cattle. Anyhow it is all in the game.'*

If we weren't on training schemes we were kept occupied on innumerable route marches. For the older people who watched silently as we went swinging by it must have seemed like a time warp for we were still singing the marching songs of the 1914-18 war, 'Mademoiselle from Armentieres', 'Pack up your Troubles', 'When this bleeding War is Over and we're back upon the dole', and the regimental march ' The Bladon Races', to mention some of the favourites. We were still thinking the last war. The sad thing was at this time so were some of the Generals. The 505 anti-tank rifle was a case in point, it needed a six pounder at least to stop a tank, as time was to show.

Scrounging now entered our way of life. To keep the large

barrack room warm there was a coal stove in the centre which heated the immediate area around it. There was never enough coal so we scrounged, a word which is covered by the phrase 'beg, borrow or steal'. It was generally the latter. To wash, one went down iron staircases which ran outside, like fire escapes, to the wash houses below where cold water was plentiful. One moved at the double from choice, or froze.

One night in the freezing barrack room a group of us were huddled around the stove. What the conversation was is lost in the mists of time but I can assure you that almost every other word would have been fuck, fucker or fucking. When quite suddenly we were facing death in a very unpleasant form. It happened in an unexpected way as these things are apt to do. One of our comrades in arms had returned to barracks as the saying is 'the worse for drink' and flopped on his bed as was normal. As far as we were concerned he was forgotten. But, for some reason best known to himself, he got up, fixed his bayonet in his rifle and with a roar of "I'll get one of you fucking bastards!" he charged. He would doubtless have managed to achieve his intention but for one small thing. Barrack rooms in machine gun training depots had three small L-shaped blocks of wood screwed to the floor, to stop the tripod moving about when it was set up in the barrack room. On one of these our comrade with arms tripped. He attempted to get up but we descended on him like a load of bricks. He was contrite the following morning and went sick with severe bruising and two black eyes. He told the M.O. he had slipped on the icy steps.

It was about this time I had a visit from my brother when the minesweeper he was serving on called into Newcastle. It was an ex trawler and one of the Northern boats, Northern Star, Northern Foam, Northern Wave etc. We had a good day together and I now remember it for the fact that as we parted we shook hands for the first time. He ended up on a flak ship which joined convoys and sailed up the Channel with them. Years later he was to tell me that they were once left behind because of engine trouble and as they were trying to sort their problem out they were spotted by a German plane. He said their boat could have been taken at sea level by a man in a rowboat with a shotgun as every gun they had pointed upwards. The German obviously thought this was his lucky day but sometime on his dive he must have realised he had made a mistake, "It must have been like flying down a gun barrel", was my brother's expression.

Some time about now I reached the peak of my Army career when I was sent on an NCOs course and ultimately made a Lance Corporal. But being an N.C.O. didn't suit me. Although I had complete confidence in myself I had no ability in passing it on. I think I got the promotion because of the results of initiative tests we were given. In these we set off in running gear, having been given a clue which led to a point where we received another clue leading to another point and so on. Interest was maintained by the fact that once back to the barracks we were finished parades for the day. I enjoyed these exercises and found them enjoyable and easy, especially as I was now a member of the Regimental cross country team. I was always one of the first, if not the first, back. The five or six others who made up the team were quite happy to follow me, the faster the better as far as they were concerned. They were particularly happy one time when I talked a bus conductor whose empty bus was just leaving its terminus out in the country, to let us travel on it for a few miles into the suburbs. We trotted into the barracks in fine style with a course record. That is my theory on why I achieved my stripe.

When I lost it I thought it bad luck but with hindsight it was probably a straight forward case of justice being done. I was in charge of a piquet of two men. We were supposed to patrol the barracks throughout the night and it was almost standard practice when on this duty to go for a drink. I was never a great drinking man in those days so probably my detail of two had a hand in persuading me to carry on the traditions of the regiment. However I was in charge and we followed standard practice by stuffing our rifles, ammunition and equipment into one of the large ovens in the cook house, which it was our duty to guard, and made to the pub.

Unfortunately that night there was an air raid and although we must have broken records in returning to the barracks when we heard the sirens, it wasn't quite sufficient. And the end result was that I reverted to the ranks. Later I was to write home and tell my parents I could have gone back to being a Lance Corporal again but it would mean me staying at the depot either as the Post Corporal or at the Dental surgery. . . what did they think I was? I might as well have stayed in civvy street.

I have one other vivid memory of that barrack room. While we were there the day was controlled by the bugle. We got up at Reveille, we answered to Cook House, Defaulters etc. We went to bed at Lights Out. But in the morning there was a wireless programme called Reveille, which was always switched on, a cheery 'life's a lark' sort of programme, absolutely ideal for jollying someone with a thick head out of his warm bed into a freezing barrack room and down snow covered steps to his wash and shave in icy cold water in about fifteen minutes flat. This programme opened with a bugle call, obviously Reveille, and it wasn't peculiar to the loud speaker in our billet – it must have started the day for every serviceman in Britain and beyond. That particular morning I, we, awoke as usual to the sound of the bugle. But it was fantastic – it wasn't Reveille, it was Lights Out. Why not? It was still dark until the black out curtains were drawn one couldn't tell if it was night or day, I must have woken in my sleep. I, we, battalions of us, blissfully turned over and snuggled down to drift back to sleep again in the silent darkness I was barely conscious when a voice brought us back to earth. "How many April fools have I caught out this morning?" The general reaction, said with sincere and deepfelt anger was, "The fucking fucker. I'd fuck him!"

Shortly after that we got the hint that we would be leaving so I hitched for the last time to my relatives. I think my uncle took my reverting to the ranks more badly than I did. He didn't say a lot at any time but he did give me his old cap badge when we parted, which said enough. Then there came a day when thirty of us, trained machine-gunners to a man, mustered on the barrack square at dawn and marched through the barrack gates, where the guard turned out for us, and went swinging through the empty streets of Newcastle to the railway station. We were on a draft to join the 4th Battalion of the Northumberlands. And I never saw a Vickers machine gun again.

CHAPTER 2

The Fourth battalion, as were all Fourth battalions, was a territorial one. Territorials were volunteers who in pre war days had put in a stipulated number of drills a year and attended a fortnights' annual camp. They also got some payment which I imagine was looked on as beer money. A company could be made up completely with men from one village. They had joined up with their 'marras' from the pit. (They always talked of pits and pitmen, never miners). Most of the N.C.O.s were deputies or foremen at the local pit and the officers were local businessmen, solicitors or accountants etc. The two villages I can remember from which companies were raised were Throckley and Newburn. This method had its drawbacks. There was one company in a Territorial battalion of the Border Regiment which had been almost completely wiped out in France. The newspaper description of Endmoor at the time was 'the village of missing men.' I remembered it because Endmoor had a Youth Hostel where I had stayed when cycling. However this wasn't going to happen to the Fourth as the losses which they had suffered in France seemed to have been made up with Londoners. The Fourth battalion's casualties had been pretty considerable in France, almost fifty percent, and after their return to England some of the Battalion, mainly married men, had volunteered to go back to the pits, but for all the new intakes it still had the feeling of a Geordie Mob and Geordies still seemed to predominate. They had a song which they sang when they had had a few drinks called The Abington Mashers. I think Abington must have been where they had their annual camp. I can remember the words well. Heaven knows, I sang them often enough. And it might tell you something about the Fourth Northumberlands.

> We are the Abington Mashers
> We go every night on the mash
> And when we can't get any beer
> It's all for the want of some cash.
> We can dance, we can sing,

We're all right, all right
When we're tight, tight, tight,
We don't give a damn for tomorrow.
What we ain't got we can borrow.
All that we require is beer, baccy and c...

Where I had joined them in Shepton Mallet in Somerset the village suited them well as they had quickly adapted to the local drink, cider, which was a fraction of the cost of beer. Some of the draft I came down with, found that out the hard way as they equated the strength with the cost.

For all their constant moaning and griping about the army few of the Geordies needed to be in it. Mining was a reserved occupation and as pitmen they were constantly being asked to return to their old jobs. I never knew one that did. It may have been what is now known as peer pressure, but that's the way it was – they soldiered on. They were now motorised infantry with Bren carriers, motorbike combinations and trucks. Their weapon was the Bren gun where, unlike the Vickers which spread its favours wide, with a Bren one bullet would more or less follow the other into the same hole. The whole battalion got a laugh about this time when we read in the papers that special units of elite troops were being formed into Recconnaisance Battalions. Overnight we became special units of elite troops and were given another cap badge. It was a design of a spear with two jagged lines coming from it. It looked like a Christmas tree. A Recconnaisance unit we may have become, but if you brainwash men to take a pride in serving in one of the oldest regiments in the army, the Fifth of Foot, you cannot expect them to accept getting put into a new regiment with a Christmas tree for a cap badge, even if you tell them they are now elite troops. It was never worn. The 50th Recconnaisance Battalion always wore the badge of the Royal Northumberland Fusiliers. As well as this, the C.O., Lt. Col. de Graz, who had come from the Rifle Brigade, always wore the cap badge of that regiment.

I was posted to 12 Platoon, Z Company, as a rifleman. It was about the norm for any infantry platoon in the British Army. The platoon leader was a Second Lieutenant Mills, sound and steady, who had been destined for the Police Force, and we had two good sergeants. Edwards, the senior one, had been a school boy international and had had a trial for Newcastle. What better accolade could one need? The other, Peachy Dunn (Dunns are often called Peachy in the army – Peachy being the Hindustani word for soon) was a sorbo rubber ball of a man. Later, when he was climbing the wire, attempting an escape from one of the prison camps in Tripoli, and his companion was shot, Peachy kept on going. The corporal, a Londoner, was known by the army meaning of his initials and it suited him, A.T. otherwise, Anti Tank Jones. The Lance Corporal, Heaney, was the instigator of a platoon joke. One of the platoon called Vic had been taking a look from a sunken road in France when he had drawn the fire of a German with a Spandau. He had come down quicker than he went up. Unfortunately it was on to Heaney's bayonet who was crouching below. He had a large scar on his behind to prove it and at appropriate times, when he was talking to girls for instance, the call would be, "Show them where you were wounded, Vic." He may have been what is now called accident prone. Later I saw one happen to him. He was on a motor-bike, riding quite close up behind a truck in which some of us were travelling. The truck straddled a large pot hole but the bike didn't, couldn't. As for Vic, there he was, gone.

The other Lance corporal was called Green and had been training for the priesthood in Ireland when

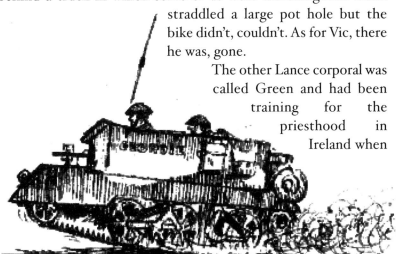

the war broke out and he decided to change his vocation.

Another in the platoon was Cranney. I once saw him crying as he fired a Bren gun and I came to the conclusion it was because of frustration that the bullets weren't coming out fast enough.

Another platoon member from Gateshead had a fancy for large women. He was a small man himself and later in towns that catered for such things, the members of the platoon that had been let out first would take it on themselves to find which brothel had the largest woman and come back and report.

I had a fight with another platoon member which the others kindly stopped. I found out later he made money by taking up the challenges: 'Stay five rounds for a Tenner' in the boxing booths that came with the travelling fairs. They would have been kinder if they had stopped it earlier. Later when we were in the Western Desert he deserted. My closest friend, marra, was called Naarden. He was Jewish, of Dutch extraction. Now a driver, he had been a London taxi driver. Brittain was another Londoner with whom I became friendly. He was in the signal section and I swopped Penguins with him. People who read books were rare.

We had been issued with two kit bags at this time, one for gear needed on voyage and one for the ship's hold. One man, Lowry by name, who was a bit of a wag, by careful packing got everything he had in one kit bag but this form of initiative was frowned on and he had to repack it in the two kit bags he had been issued with. He did as ordered but both kit bags seemed to be half empty.

As a whole the platoon were great moaners. But we had the champion, who was nicknamed Minnie, but a prodigious worker, moaning all the time of course. We had one who would now be called gay, but he was generally accepted and in later days he went mincing out under fire to bring a wounded man in. The Geordies and the Londoners soon fused together and the only time there was any obvious difference, except for their dialects, was when they were digging in. The Londoners stood up to do it but the Geordies squatted down on their "hunkers" as if they were still working in a low seam down the pit. They did it much faster as well.

The training schemes in the Battalion had a far more realistic approach to life. We were told that a good soldier should never stand when he could sit, sit when he could lie and lie when he could sleep. The 4th were naturals. On one night exercise we came to a halt in what was pretty near a swamp - we were standing in about an inch of water. The order came back "Make yourself comfortable, we may be here for sometime." After a few entirely reasonable comments on this order we set about doing just that. In a remarkably short time 12 Platoon was asleep, we were sitting in our tin helmets, packs keeping head and shoulders above water level, rifles between our legs and only our feet, already wet, in the water. As I have said 'naturals'.

I wrote of another night scheme in a letter home:

"Our section, we were seven, got the thrill of the night. We were supposed to be on a recce patrol and were crossing a golf links about 15 yards from the club house, all of us wrapped in our own thoughts, when all of a sudden someone shouted "HALT!" and we could hear a rifle being cocked. Out of habit we all flopped on the ground and froze. It was a Home Guard post and I tried to hide behind a blade of grass. Then the guard commander turned out. 'What be it?' and we could hear him as plain as anything. 'There's someone out there,' replied the guard but neither of them would come out to see if there was. None of us would move in case he heard us and let drive and none of us would call out who we were because if the lads got to know we had been caught napping by the Home Guard we would never live it down. Apart from the seven in our section, you are the only ones to know, we were nearly captured by the Home Guard."

I had two strokes of luck when I was in Shepton Mallet, a large one and a small one. The platoon was based in the upper and ground floor of a large building. I was on the upper floor when some absent-minded rifleman below, who was cleaning his rifle, pressed the trigger and found out he had left a round up the spout. There were two of us on the floor above who later debated who was the luckiest because the bullet went between us. The other stroke of luck was when I was sent on embarkation leave. During this leave I read in the paper that there had been an accident during a demonstration of three inch mortars at some army camp and there had been some casualties. It was only when I returned I found they had been in my company, some in my platoon. Thirty three of them injured and four killed. The mortar bomb had gone straight up about twenty feet and then straight down. They hadn't stood a chance. On a much broader front there was good news. In June 1941 Hitler declared war on Russia and we were no longer alone. Stalin, or Uncle Joe as he was known to the troops, was now on our side.

My last memory of Shepton Mallet is of a village dance. I won't say it was equivalent to the ball before Waterloo, nevertheless they must have had something in common. Mine also had repercussions that went on a bit. I had danced with one attractive girl with whom I had struck up some accord and when I saw her again, or thought I did, I asked her again for a dance and away we went. I tried to pick up the conversation where we had left off but for some reason she didn't seem able to. Nevertheless she was obviously enjoying herself. The dance was almost over when I saw my first partner, my present partner's identical twin. They were identically dressed, all was made clear. It was an innocent joke they must have played often. I became friendly with them and all was going well until the same thing happened with a sergeant out of our company. Unfortunately when he discovered what was happening I was laughing with his earlier partner and he assumed I was in on the joke. From then on if there was a fatigue party needed my name was invariably on it. After a few weeks things went back to normal. And months later I found that the platoon had noticed this sergeant had a down on me and hinted to him that it was often an unlucky thing thing to do if you were going into action and someone had a grudge against you.

That was the thing about a platoon. It looked after its own. I wouldn't say it was effusive. I suppose it was a term of mutual insurance but it was nice to have.

The draft from Fenham which arrived to make our numbers up after the incident with the mortar had barely arrived before we were off to Newport and the Arundel Castle. This wasn't what it sounded like. It belied its name. It was a troopship.

CHAPTER 3

The sailing of the Arundel Castle was a quiet affair with no bands or flags or people to wave as our lines were cast off, just a few blase dockside workers who had seen it all before. There was however a small incident that sent us off in a good mood. Gradually the gangplanks that had connected to the land had been removed until there was only one left and down this went half a dozen military police who had been helping with the control of the embarkation. Not the most popular of men, there were lots of ribald comments aimed at them but they ignored them. Like the dockies, they had probably seen and heard it all before. Then, in one of those odd lulls that one can get in such a hubbub, a voice rang out as clear as a bell, "There go the rats deserting the ship!" It was ignored by them all except the last one who turned around, his face furious and as red as the top of his cap. He glared up at the thousands of faces looking down at him and we could see his voice mouthing the word "Bastard." There was a huge roar of approval in reply on the realisation that the shaft had gone home.

The Arundel Castle sailed from Newport to join our convoy and initially we of the 50th Northumbrian Division seemed extremely well looked after, with corvettes, destroyers, a light cruiser and flying boats constantly in attendance. As we got further into our voyage - it was 12,000 miles - leaving grey sea for blue our attendants were not so obvious. Everyone knew there was danger from U Boats but I cannot recollect anyone being concerned. It was a case of ignorance is bliss.

During daylight one could see the ships of the convoy and its escorts, and somewhere beyond them we all knew there were U Boats. We lost one ship but it was only when the survivors were spread out amongst the rest of the convoy at Freetown that we knew it had happened. The ones we got on the Arundel Castle were RAF ground crew. I've thought since, but not then, that being torpedoed must have been a terrible way to go. We ourselves were crammed way down in the bowels of the ship with one more to a cabin than there were bunks, so we ran a roster of who slept on the floor. To hear the crump of a torpedo and feel the ship list as the seas surged through that seething rabbit warren of crowded passage ways was something that never entered our heads. We were young and indestructible and above all else, unimaginative.

In fact, if we wanted to we could sleep on deck. Most of the RAF survivors did. But there was a drawback in that the ship's crew washed the deck down daily at a very early hour and they had no inhibitions about using the hose pipe to wake you up. The half hour extra kip, even if in a rabbit warren a few decks below sea level, won every time.

During the day we were kept busy with lectures that the Army thought might come in handy - lectures on gas, and VD (a cause of more casualties than those inflicted by the enemy, though, unlike casualties, there was a three week cure. This lecture had some horrendous coloured slides to go with it). There was also Aircraft Recognition, map reading and Physical Training which consisted of runs around the deck. And fatigues . . . in those pre-dishwashing-machine days there was an awful lot of washing up. And because of my dancing with those twins I did a lot of it. Fortunately, as I found out later, it was round about this time that 12 Platoon pointed out to the Sergeant the potentially dangerous side effects of going into action with someone who bore you a grudge and the time I spent on fatigues eased off.

Card schools kept many occupied. Vast amounts of money changed hands because platoons would get together to bank one player whom they considered good enough to be entrusted with their money. So there would be intense and critical audiences with a vested interest in the outcome of a game and the fluctuation of their fortunes. The combined week's wages of most of a platoon could hang on the turn of a card. This was one area where the ship's crew and the army met because there would always be a white-shirted figure, and his backers, amongst the khaki.

For the ones who didn't gamble there was always the Housey housey. But for me one of my strongest memories of the Arundel Castle was the suppers. Food wise they were pretty basic, simply hard ship's biscuits, chunks of cheddar cheese and mugs of hot sweet cocoa but above all it was unlimited and as we always seemed to be hungry this was a tremendous attraction. It was served on the deck on a help your self basis and to make yourself comfortable with a couple of friends and unlimited food to go at what more could a squaddie ask for? .... life seemed very pleasant and to round it off there were the sing songs. These were not regular affairs - they just happened. And to lie sprawled on the deck completely replete in the warm dusk and sing your heart out in those nostalgic sentimental songs of the day . . . as I have said, memorable.

Although the threat of U-boats did not cause us much loss of sleep in a metaphorical sense, they did in fact cause it physically as we had to stand submarine watches. As a duty it wasn't very onerous. We had to stand on the upper deck, normally officer only country and out of bounds to other ranks, and look out for submarines. There was one particular submarine watch I will always remember. There were a few nurses on board who messed with the officers, and romances between them were inevitable. By the nature of their circumstances these romances must have been incredibly intense, with the heightened awareness of it all, the man going to war, and death lurking just beyond the farthest boats of the convoy. But the numbers on board ensured that a couple was never alone. On the upper deck of a cruise liner, a spot designed for romance, they leaned on the ship's rails shoulder pressed to shoulder, looking down at the ship's shadow sliding over the smooth moonlit sea. And, as if to add to their longing, they could hear, carried faintly over the warm tropical night from one of accompanying ships, the singing, accompanied by the inevitable mouth organ, of its nostalgic passengers:

"We'll meet again

Don't know where, don't know when,

But I know we'll meet again some..."

Distance lent enchantment to those rude voices. Even I thought that and I knew the couple leaning on the rail ten or twelve yards from me would have been more enchanted still if I had been as distant from them as the singers were. Whereas I on my part was wishing myself off watch and down below, though probably not with the same ardour as they.

We had one passenger on the ship who was the odd one out in many respects. This was the Emperor of Abbyssinia. He was also known as the Lion of Judah but for all his grandiloquent title he was a tiny bearded man who always wore a black cloak and we often saw him walking around the upper decks for exercise. Although we did not appreciate it then, he was the first of the monarchs deposed by the Axis forces to be returned to his throne.

The convoy called in at Durban and the welcome from the English speaking South Africans was fantastic. Nothing was too good for us. I say English speaking with reason because South Africa came into the war by the narrowest of margins, one vote I believe, the English speaking South Africans voting to join Britain in the war and the Afrikaaners voting to stay out, though both sections realised they had to show a united front against the coloured population. Mickey Naarden, with his knowledge of Dutch, could pick up what Africaans speakers were saying. They may have had the same coloured skin as the English speakers, but they didn't think alike. There was one incident which could have turned unpleasant until it was smoothed over by obviously pleased English speakers. It happened on a bus where a group of us from the platoon were travelling. Mickey was puffing away at his pipe beside a group of vociferous Afrikaaners who were obviously finding a lot to laugh at. Mickey finished his smoke, tapped out his pipe and, turning to the rest of us, said, "Do you know what these Boer bastards are saying about us?" Then he told us. The Afrikaaners were flabbergasted that their conversation had been understood and as we rose to show them that what we thought about them the English speaking passengers, though pleased, moved between us and talked us out of it as the Afrikkaners left en mass. Whites fighting whites wasn't the done thing.

I think all the South Africans even then, fifty odd years ago, realised they had problems to come and did everything they could to sell us on the attractions of South Africa. To them, out numbered ten to one by coloured people, the more white people that went there after the war the better. To show us what the natives were like there was one place I think everyone was shown. It was a huge cage, probably covering the area of a couple of tennis courts, with thick wooden bars, and inside there were rows of heavy wooden tables and long wooden forms bolted to the floor. This was one of the places where the natives were allowed to buy drink, kaffir beer, and get drunk. And they certainly did that. It was Rabelasian. There aren't many people who have seen a drunken orgy but most of the troops that stopped at Durban have. The intention was to show us what a sub-standard species the natives were. But we went to a fair number of parties when we were there, and the only difference was that white South Africans, and us, got drunk in private.

I think it was the regular thing that when a convoy came into Durban the authorities for some reason or another put on a military parade. It was the parade I was involved in that brought home to me the power of music - martial music in this case. It was hot, and we all knew there were far, far better things we could be doing and would rather be doing, swimming and drinking to mention only two, than marching along the baking hot roads of Durban. It was as we were coming along the side of the town hall before before entering the main square that the band struck up. It was the regimental march, Bladon Races. A far cry from our passing out parade on the barrack square at Fenham Barracks, but we had forgotten nothing. As the strains of the regimental march filled the square we came together as one. The Royal Northumberlands, the Fifth of Foot, swung past the saluting base like a huge machine, brain-washed perhaps, but eight hundred men thinking and acting as one gives a marching column a larger life of its own. It kept us going until we fell out at the docks. Only then did we notice it was still baking hot.

I am afraid I let the white South Africans down on my last night in Durban, but fortunately few were there to see it. It was in the main due to Cape brandy. There were a few of us on our last night in Durban returning to the boat in a convoy of rickshaws. The large bedecked Zulu who was pulling the one I was in was padding along nicely and quietly with his plumes nodding as he

In such a vehicle I nearly killed myself when I reversed roles with the owner whilst under the influence. I am on the right.

must have done many times before, when I got the idea I would like to try pulling the rickshaw. There was a lot of argument from him, but a lot of encouragement from the others of the platoon and I finally ended up in the shafts. After getting what I thought was the right balance, I felt I was taking huge floating strides, though the brandy may have helped - and also the fact that we were on a downhill slope. The critical moment came when the automatic signals at the cross roads at the bottom changed to red. Army boots haven't the traction of bare feet. Fortunately no damage was done and I finished the journey to the Arundel Castle asleep in the back of the rickshaw.

Aden was our next port of call and we had a good idea now as to where we were going. It was while we were here leaning on the rails and watching the constant movement of shipping that we saw the battleship Barham leaving the harbour. She dwarfed every thing else. It was an impressive and stirring sight and with her white ensign and signal flags fluttering, her crew lining her decks and the sun glinting on the instruments of the marine band, a memorable one. We could hear the music coming across the harbour to us and we knew the words

"Hearts of oak are our ships,
Jolly tars are our men..."

Memorable. But her luck ran out a few months later when she was hit by three torpedoes and went down in as many minutes, taking five hundred of her jolly tars with her.

She has barely passed when we saw an example of the minutae of war. A corvette was passing below us and as we looked down on her a matalot appeared on deck and started walking aft. Someone, three or four down the rail from me, gave a call. "Hey, Joe!" The matalot stopped and looked up. There must have been thousands of faces looking down at him a waving arm drew his attention. "Hello, Bob," was his reply. The corvette continued on its way and they kept looking at each other and waving. 'Who the hell was that?" came the question. "My fucking brother," came the reply.

Our voyage ended in Port Tewfik. Here we saw the war at closer hand. As we came in to dock a destroyer slid slowly past us, but not shipshape and Bristol fashion as the ones we had seen in Aden. This one had torn and twisted plates, guns blown askew and numerous ragged holes in her superstructure. She had been in the wars ...We had arrived.

CHAPTER 4

We disembarked at Port Tewfik and were billetted in a transit camp. And here we discovered the truth in the saying that East is East and West is West and never the twain shall meet. This was due to the latrines which were large wooden ten-holers with a hessian screen round them. We shared these latrines with an Indian unit and we found that there was a fundamental difference in our approach to this fundamental act. The East squats but the West sits. The West had no objection to this except that the East squatted where the West sat with their boots or sandals on and didn't always hit the hole. Later it became so obvious which was the best and we were soon squatting with the best of them. But just off the boat, our knees still white, we were incensed. Fortunately the Indians moved on and we were allowed to discover the error of our ways and the advantage of theirs in our own time.

It was in this camp I also saw our first Australians and found they also had a different way of doing things from us. I was in a canteen where a group of Australians were drinking when an Australian officer came in and said "I want six men for a fatigue." The reply was prompt. "The first six you catch you can have." The officer was more than up to it and quick on the uptake had grabbed his six before they had started reacting. But they went willingly and on good terms. Despite their individualistic attitude to army ways, or perhaps because of it, the Australians as I found later were a close second to the New Zealanders on the Germans' league table of opponents, and the Australian 9th Division had the name of being one of the best in the desert. Years later I read the memoirs of a German infantry man who told of his drill instructor making them lie prone on the ground as he walked over them. They also made good soldiers so it is debatable as to which is the best method. The British County Regiments came third on the Germans list, and must have fallen about midday between the two training methods.

For a long time I was under the impression that there were no small Australians until I was told that when the war broke out their recruiting offices were inundated and could barely cope. To stave off the rush the volunteers were told it was no good them coming unless they were 5' 10" or over. I think there was some truth in this because until fresh drafts started coming out you seldom saw a small Aussie.

It was at this transit camp that there was nearly an international incident. The name Transit camp is self explanatory and because the troops were only there for a short time whilst in transit the normal parades were greatly reduced, in fact the first parade in this type of camp was cook house, breakfast, so that one could sleep much longer than normal. Or would have except for the one man, the local muzzein who traditionally called the faithful to prayer at dawn from the minaret overlooking the camp. The drawback was, besides waking up the faithful, he also woke up a few hundred disgruntled troops, many with thick heads, in the process. One of them put the wishes of hundreds into action when he stopped the muzzein in full cry with a couple of shots above his head. There was hell to play about this but the inquiries didn't get far as there were no witnesses. Everyone said they had been asleep.

From this camp three trucks from the battalion left every night for those who wanted to go into the town. The first left at 18.00 hours, the next at 18.30 hours and then one at 19.00 hours. They were thirty hundredweight trucks and probably had twenty men on each. At the end of the evening these same three trucks repeated the procedure, leaving at half hour intervals to return to camp. But this time the first two trucks to leave the town invariably travelled back half empty and the last one would be choc a bloc with tanked-up Fusiliers, some squashed inside, some hanging outside and some sitting on the mudguards. So when the truck hit an unlit Arab truck parked by the side of the road, it was those on the mudguard that took the brunt - one killed (one of the original Abington Mashers) and about three seriously injured. I was lucky as I had missed the last truck and was making my unsteady way back alone and on foot when I was picked up by a truck from some other unit and dropped at the camp gates.

The morning after I was detailed off for the funeral party.

The army has had a lot of experience and is good at these sort of affairs, and like everything else in a soldier's life it is all laid down in King's Rules and Regulations. What I remember was the contrast. It was a solemn and moving parade with the bugler starting at 'Reveille' and going on call after call until the sad evocative notes of 'Lights Out' brought to an end the bugle calls of a soldier's day. Then Wham! - the band struck up the rousing strains of the march Colonel Bogey and we were away swinging back to camp. He was dead and buried and gone and it was over.

A result of this death was that the Battalion post bag increased considerably in the next few weeks with anxious letters from parents and families to other men in the Battalion. Obviously an official letter had been sent to the parents with news of the death and the news that one of the 4th had been killed on active service - easily confused with killed in action - had spread concern through the villages in which the battalion had been raised.

I wrote home about this time.

'Writing this just before we move from heaven knows where to the same place. I will not be sorry to leave ; here for we are pestered with flies, ants, mosquitoes, heat and the sand but taken on the whole I've enjoyed it. This is the first letter I have written here and the reason why is the flies. It seems a queer thing to say but it is a fact flies pester you so much you have to keep flicking them off so you are unable to write. But this afternoon we got issued with mosquito nets and that allowed me to start this letter. Adding a bit while we stop on our journey, left our camp yesterday at 06.30 after getting up at 04.00 arrived at this place, a big town, yesterday dinner time almost dead beat. Mick and I did not get to bed until late as we had hitch hiked into Ishmalia and when our convoy started I went to sleep and according to Mick I nearly lost my life as he went to sleep at the wheel and nearly went into the canal. Anyway we swopped over and he slept and I drove...... I got to a French Catholic canteen dance and enjoyed myself even if I cannot speak French. An air raid broke up the dance so off I went campward and had just reached there as things got lively and I dived under a railway truck which I found later was loaded with ammunition. Eventually I reached our truck and we, and the ants, just lay underneath while we watched the display, the best I've seen. Between our two front

wheels as I lay on my stomach I could count twelve searchlights, four heavy ack ack guns, ten light, and see scores of tracers from L.M.G.s and with flaming onions, it was a real fireworks display. The truck got hit five times with shrapnel, it was a good thing we were underneath. When the boys came back they told us they had dropped a lot of incendiary bombs on the town and all the townspeople did was run about crying and shouting. Anyway on the whole it was an interesting day'.... I finished the letter 'Sometimes you starve and you have to open the tin of bully you nicked and share it with your pals while the next meal you grumble because food is wasted.. Sometime you are broke because you have not been paid then the next time you get all your back pay and you feel like a millionaire with all your notes. (They have notes for twopence halfpenny here). Our chief trouble is ants. I have over fifty bites on one arm and they are the same density all over my body, too many to count and they come up like heat lumps and all you want to do is scratch and scratch and scratch all day, nearly as bad as the flies. Anyway that's the lot and if you think I am complaining don't believe it, this army is tops. It has given me some grand times. You cannot believe what it is like to drop in on some new town with a bit of money and a few pals and let things happen. And, they do. Anyway for the time, Cheerio Mick.'

Hindsight being what it is, I realise now that as we had been lying under our truck we had been watching a wasted asset. The gun of the desert was without a doubt the German 88mm, designed as an anti aircraft gun. It had been pressed into service as an anti tank gun in an emergency and when used with armour piercing shells the Germans had immediately realised its potential. As far as the German gunners were concerned it only had one drawback, this was its height which meant it needed a lot of digging in. In an anti-aircraft gun this was of little consequence. Height or not it wreaked havoc among the British armour, the tank killer par excellence until the war ended, and was the deciding factor in many a battle. We had just watched its British equivalent, the 3.7. anti-aircraft gun which, together with its crews, was under-utilised throughout the war in the desert. With the German 88mm as an example, its potential as a tank killer was often pointed out but to no avail. It saw the war out pointing to the sky. The German saying that to get on in the Army you need a modicum of stupidity can be applied to all armies.

The powers that be then thought that Hitler might be carried away with his success in Crete and attempt to take Cyprus. To anticipate this the 150th Brigade, of which we were a part, were embarked for Cyprus. It was to be a pleasant but useless interlude. It was only after the war that it was found that for the Germans Crete had been a Pyhrric victory and so great had been their losses - 6000, over fifty per cent of their elite force, the paratroopers of 1st German Airborne killed - that they never used airborne troops again. It was for this reason that Malta was never attacked by airborne troops. And if Malta had fallen the war in the Middle East may have had a different outcome.

I was lucky enough to be on the advance party going to Cyprus. Lucky because all small detachments away from the battalion were much more relaxed. I was even more lucky on the trip out. I had bedded down for the night under one of the life boats of the small cargo vessel we were travelling on and during the night the cargo, our vehicles, shifted. The end result was that the vessel heeled over to quite a considerable extent and I awoke to find myself looking down at the sea. The only thing that had kept me from slipping overboard as the boat had listed during the night was about four inches of toe rail.

We arrived at our destination, a largish village called Vatilli, late in the evening. We were tired but Mickey Naarden and myself realised that the village would never again be as it was then so when the others turned in we, tired as we were, went out. Life goes on much later in the Mediterranean climate so there were of plenty of people about, as curious about us as we were about them, and there was a restaurant open. There was no menu but we were shown into the kitchen and the proprietor started lifting the lids off pans for us to make our choice. What we had I wrote down in a letter home. *'The meal was lamb, beans and dumplings. We made signs-that we would like to wash our hands and a shy young girl came out with an earthenware pot and poured water over them, then gave us a harsh towel to dry them on. It was Biblical.'* And we were right, it was never like that again.

When the rest of the company finally joined us, it had a little contretemps which turned out all for the best. The area we were allotted was in a wood of eucalyptus trees and trucks came in from all directions. The only occupant in the wood was a donkey and for a time he was a source of amusement as he galloped about in a panic generated by the unusual noise and movement of vehicles, until he or she finally disappeared and was forgotten. Throughout the day we never saw anyone from the village until quite late in the afternoon when a small girl appeared. She was obviously scared stiff and near to tears, but no one could make out what was wrong until she put both hands up by the side of her head like ears. The donkey. Every one felt guilty and everyone seemed to have an idea as to where it had gone, and off they went in pursuit. In a very short time the girl had the choice of about twenty donkeys and a few mules for good measure. They had been found everywhere, grazing or standing in the shade in the seemingly deserted village.

The owners, we later discovered, were too scared to tell us nay. Fortunately our next visitor was the village schoolmaster, an English speaker. All was explained and the anxious owners of the rustled animals came to collect their livestock. This incident broke the ice with the villagers and from then on all was well.

There was another incident caused by the apprehension of the villagers to troops when we were moved to another village. In this case we were having a game of football on the outskirts and had made a couple of makeshift goal posts. One was a pole we had stuck in the ground and the other was a roughly made wooden box we had found propped up against a wall. As it was about six foot long and could balance upright it was ideal for the purpose. Soon after the game started we attracted a solitary spectator who took up his position behind the goal posts and after a time the goal keeper realised it wasn't our skill that was the attraction but the goal post. The end result was he was given permission to take it away and he left with it over his shoulder. Shortly afterwards we saw a small group of villagers leave the village following one of their two wheeled carts on which was the box we had been using for a goal post. It now had a body in it and we realised that we had been using the communal coffin. After a time the mourners returned and the communal coffin was propped up again where we had originally found it but this time we left it there.

With Micky Naarden in Cyprus with a ubiquitous 15 cwt Bedford, Millie II. Millie I was Naarden's wife.

It was here we found Cypriot traditions and army traditions went hand in hand. We had by now become quite friendly with the villagers and would be invited to their homes and particularly weddings. Traditionally these lasted three days, the day before the wedding, the day of the wedding and the day after. In the army our life was also divided into three, being on guard for twenty four hours, standing to for the next twenty four hours and the third day you were off duty. It meant that every one in the platoon could attend the wedding. Our contribution to the wedding feast was invariably the same, tinned pilchards in tomato sauce. Fortunately this food, which came up regularly in the rations, the Cypriots considered a delicacy.

I wrote home about guard duty.... *'If you are on eight till ten you have plenty of company as the boys return. The sober ones and that is by far the majority stop for a chat and a smoke before turning in, the drunken ones come back singing such like songs as the Red Flag and 'The Irish Rebel", both prohibited. That's why they sing them. During the night it is like England in some respects, generally you can hear a baby crying someplace, stray dogs sniffing around and as in England heavy transport moves at night so here heavily laden camels with swaying loads pad past while bats with their curious screeches make you start and the everlasting chirp of the crickets continues all night long. About four thirty the village starts to awake and mule carts start chattering out of the village, streams of them, cocks start crowing and native labourers with their picks and shovels and baskets start off to their work and although it is pitch dark at five thirty you can hear the clatter of the dixies as the cooks get cracking and the roar of their stoves. At six it is light and the women of the village come to the wells with their jars and ropes on which they lower the jars down into the well. At seven its breakfast, at eight you start thawing out, at nine the sun gets up, at ten you start sweating and it goes on.'*

There was one letter I wrote when I was in Vattili which I had to tear up as unsuitable for home consumption. It happened because two of the platoon got word that they had become fathers and everyone who was off duty went out with them to help them with the traditional ceremony of "wetting the baby's bottom." As wine was the equivalent of three halfpence a bottle this was done in no mean manner. We staggered, rolled back to the billets in fine style and for some reason I decided to write a letter home before I turned in and the morning after when I saw it I tore it up. It wasn't as much as reading between the lines because there were only about four of them but the huge sprawled letters that wandered drunkenly across the page told all. Although it could

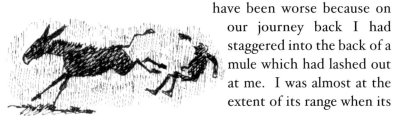

have been worse because on our journey back I had staggered into the back of a mule which had lashed out at me. I was almost at the extent of its range when its hoof made contact with my chest. Otherwise my mother would have received one of the army's all embracing forms with a tick at the box denoting Killed on Active Service, and my companions an excuse for a drunken wake.

We did have one drink related accident when we were in these billets which most of us heard but no one saw. Our billet was a two storied affair and the method of getting to the upper level where we slept was by a wooden ladder, and it was our regular practice to try to mount this ladder without using our hands, relying solely on balance. There were two schools of thought, the quick dash or the slow balancing act. We were woken up this particular night by the singing of probably the oldest man the platoon - he was probably in his mid thirties - and he was one to whom drink meant a lot. Cyprus with its cheap drink suited him well. We all heard him fumbling around at the bottom of the ladder and then the quick bump bump bump as he attempted a quick dash. He almost made it and then we heard the crash as, too fuddled to grab for the ladder, he landed at the bottom of it, battered and bruised but not broken. Although it caused him pain then it may have been that drink saved his life. I was told that later in the desert some members of the Platoon, including him, came across a deserted truck that had obviously belonged to a Padre and which was carrying the drink for the officer's mess . All except him had taken a bottle and moved on but he could not bear to leave it so he had been left on his own knocking it back. He would have realised he would be taken prisoner but doing it in the manner he preferred and would indubitably have been in fine voice.

Of all the guards I ever did in the army there was one I did in Cyprus which stays in the mind because of the company I had, a hedgehog. It was a brilliant moonlight night and time seemed to be going ever so slowly when this hedgehog came snuffling along on his nocturnal travels. I touched him with my bayonet and immediately he curled up in a ball and I waited patiently until he regained his courage and set off on his travels. Again I touched him with my bayonet and he curled up again and so with me keeping him in my sphere of influence with my bayonet the two slow hours of my guard pleasantly passed . At the end of my guard I rolled him back into the ditch from where he had come.

It was when we were in Cyprus that the Platoon got engaged. This happened through one its members, an ex London taxi driver called Doc Brown. He was a conscript and if he had not been so bloody minded he would probably have been made an NCO as he was well up to the job. Short cropped hair was the norm but Doc always had his head completely shaved. He affected a very large and well cared for black moustache and always wore his cap right on the top of his head, dead centre. It looked to say the least unmilitary and he knew it and didn't care and there was nothing in King's rules and regulations against it. It was a gesture. How he got the platoon engaged came about when he was reading a newspaper which had been used as a wrapping for some parcel he had received from home. In the classified columns there was an insertion from a man asking for a female pen friend. He had a reserved job and wanted a steady relationship. Doc decided that 12 Platoon, 'Z' Company of the 4th Northumberlands, would fit the bill perfectly and replied on their behalf. Hilda was the name he decided on, not as old fashioned then as it is now. We, she, he wrote that all letters should be addressed to her, care of her father Sergeant Edwards, (our platoon Sargeant), a regular soldier stationed out here in the Middle East. The first letter continued to say that she, having had to live in army quarters for so long, had seen so many soldiers that she was sick and fed up with the sight of men in uniform. This was obviously the right approach and from them on the affair prospered. Mail took on a new attraction. 12 Platoon looked forward to the letters for Hilda and they were read out to everyone's interest. Likewise the replies from her were also read out and Doc was always open to suggestions or improvements before they were posted. In answer to a not unreasonable request for a photograph someone managed to get a very attractive photograph from a girl in a brothel. In a remarkably short time there was an engagement. I was told that after I had left the platoon an engagement ring was received and sold and drunk, and if it had not been for the high rate of casualties that 12 Platoon was to suffer shortly who knows where it would all have ended.

Doc, like all conscripts, would at times remind you that he was here because he had to be, whereas I and the other volunteers, which included the original Abington Mashers, were there because we wanted to be there. Nevertheless they never used that argument to get out of any the jobs going. I probably remember him well because of a meal we had together. It was in a very crowded restaurant. The proprietor told us there was no room but Doc saw a small empty table about four foot by eighteen inches with a plant on it and talked the proprietor into putting the table in the corridor which led to the kitchen. Here, away from the rest of the other diners, we had our meal as a steady stream of waiters passed and repassed. Doc soon struck up a rapport with them and as one would expect we had fantastic service. Others might have looked on this as second best but not Doc. Sometime during the meal Doc said ,"You will probably have a lot of restaurant meals in your life, Mick, and if we had got a table in the restaurant this would just have been one of them, but not now. This is one you will always remember." And he was right.

There was another meal of sorts I remember that happened in Cyprus. We had returned from some scheme, famished as always, and when the dixies of food appeared their contents quickly disappeared. We were standing around in the dusk scraping out our mess tins when someone appeared from one of the other platoons and asked us if we were complaining about the food. On what ground we asked? And we were shown that nestling in every bean that had been in the stew there was a small grub. There were the expected remarks, "So that's why it tasted so good," but the end result was that we borrowed a mess tin of the stew from one of the other platoons because we had none left ourselves and complained as indignantly as the rest . The Orderly Officer agreed with our complaints and as we were issued with another meal we were well satisfied with life that evening.

Another culinary experience we had was when about a dozen of us were sent off on a detachment and as we were too small in numbers to warrant a cook we had to cook in turns.

Because of this we found we had hidden talent. One of our members had been a chef at Fortnum and Masons before being called up but as he had no inclination to cook in the army he had kept quiet about his capabilities. It was professional pride that was his undoing because on the day it was his turn to cook he turned the inevitable bully and biscuits, with the addition of a few herbs he acquired, into savoury sausages, the taste of such we had long forgotten. His momentary lapse in a manner of speaking cooked his goose. We insisted he cooked every day and on our return to the battalion we spread his capabilities wide and shortly afterwards he was transferred to the kitchen of the officer's mess.

CHAPTER 5

Early in November 1941 our pleasant way of life ended . We left Cyprus on a mine laying cruiser HMS Abdiel. She was one of four sisterships of which only one survived the war, the Abdiel herself going down when she struck a mine entering Taranto harbour. The Abdiel landed us at Haifa and off we went to the Western Desert, what was generally known as "the blue". We got a laugh en route when we heard of the breakdown of one of the new vehicles we had been issued with. The trouble was traced to a pair of socks which some well wisher had stuffed down alongside the engine and which had ultimately arrived in the fan belt. The socks when found were useless for their original purpose and a note was found which when pieced together was from the knitter of the socks wishing the finder well and exhorting him to "give them hell." Her ears must have burnt for a little time.

Prior to the Battalion having been dispatched up 'the blue', some of the officers had been sent on ahead to see what it was all about. One of these was the type that I thought the epitome of an officer - tall, dark and with the arrogant self-confidence acquired at a public school. He had a thick dark moustache to give a touch of maturity to his young face and an accent designed to 'rally the ranks when the Gatlin jammed'. However his warrior like looks belied him. What ever he saw up in the blue he did not like. He wasted no time on his return on finding out that he was seriously short sighted. You can keep few secrets in a Battalion with batmen, medical orderlies and mess stewards about. He wanted out, to go home and the quicker the better. And he did. He made it back to England and we heard later via letters that he had become a desert expert, as one would expect of a man of his character.

My first actual view of the enemy was quite a surprise. I was on a patrol and as it happened I was the man on 'point', that is, the one on his own in front. All armies have them and they are expendable. All of a sudden there they were, a truck full of Italians driving straight at me. They were all armed and had a small gun mounted on the truck and I can only assume they had been waiting in a wadi until they considered the moment was right to surrender - which happened to coincide with me arriving on the scene. As it was obvious what they wanted, I pointed to the rest of the section behind me and they in turn pointed to the getaway man behind them. And if they kept on the same bearing they would eventually arrive at where they wanted to be, which was Cairo. We thought this a great joke In time to come we found boxes of medals in an Italian quarter master's stores which had been optimistically struck for the Italians' entry into Cairo. We gave some to the Italians we had captured at the time, still thinking it was a bit of a joke, but I think in the end they had the last laugh . I should imagine almost all of those Italians went home after the war was over which is more than can be said for some of the jokers who gave them those medals.

Although the enemy in this case had come a long way to surrender it is patrols such as this, keeping in touch with the enemy, that are the basis of a battalion's work and which forms the basis of what goes down on the situation map. Later there was another patrol, at night this time, when we got more than a surprise. We were padding along when we dropped down into a slight declivity and came across a cigarette glowing in the darkness. It may have been small but it fairly shrieked at us. There are others afoot in the night! I lived from second to second for quite some time. Later there were jokes - "I felt like taking a drag at it myself." But not at the time.

In those days when news reports mentioned that British Forces had made contact with the enemy this was often the way it had happened. In wars all men are expendable but on some days, the day he is on "point" for instance, he is more expendable than other days. And of course he could be luckier sometimes when he is the last man of the patrol with the self explanatory title of "getaway man."

About this time we were involved in an incident which brought home to us what the phrase fortunes of war meant. The various Platoons in the Company were sent to the coast on a roster so that we could have a swim and it was the luck of 12 platoon that we arrived on the beach at the same time as scores of Italian corpses. They had obviously been on a troopship that had been torpedoed and their bloated bodies straining at their life jackets were lining the shore, with more arriving by the minute. The swimming party ended up as a burial detail and the basis of a Battalion joke, "Fall in 12 Platoon for a bathing parade - bring your shovels. "

We had a comfortable time in this area. We had been issued with sections of canvas which when two were buttoned together became a tent. The drawback here was that a tent was above the ground and we very quickly dug down and used the canvas sections solely as the roof. They all had the traditional names, The Ritz, Claridges, etc. The one I shared was the Midland after Manchester's finest. I wrote home about it at the time. *"It is a snug hole alright, it is sandproof, windproof and rainproof, the only thing it won't stop is the Orderly Sergeant."* The best one by far was one occupied by a Gateshead man called Lowry. The reason why his shelter was exceptional was that from somewhere he had acquired a large square of amazingly coloured silk, mainly red with a vivid and exotic pattern swirling about it. He could squeeze this sheet of silk almost to nothing but once spread out it transformed his hole in the sand into something quite extraordinary. When one ducked down into his burrow one was staggered by the contrast. Outside a cold featureless desert, down below a feeling of warmth, comfort, opulence. As was said at the time "like a fucking brothel." And that is no doubt where it had been acquired. He had also acquired a primus stove so tea was always on tap. It was a popular and often a very crowded hole in the desert.

It was in this area we spent a rainy, quiet and traditional army Christmas . Traditional because the platoon officer and N.C.O.s served the Christmas dinner, quiet because we had only one tin of beer each. But it was the New Year that I remember because of what can best be described in army parlance as self inflicted injuries. We were fortunate that in our area we had a large dug-out about twenty by twenty feet, dug by some former inhabitants of the area. In this we had a couple of trestle tables, some forms to sit on, an oil lamp and, because of an expedition to an advanced fighter aerodrome, beer and plenty of it. It all happened when the New Year's Eve celebrations were over. Someone got the idea of having them again at the same time as in England. I think an hour and twenty minutes later. It was during this time the tables were knocked over, the light went out and most made for the steps to the outside. The first two men up were a couple of good friends called Main and Cole, and for some reason best known to themselves, though I have no doubt the drink helped, they started knocking out the ones that followed them, one hitting them over the head with a lump of timber and the other one dragging them away. I think they clobbered four or five before it was realised what was happening. However it could have been worse as besides flares going up there was live ammunition flying around as well and no one got hit with that.

It was about this time that we must have got familiar with manhandling sand channels. These were a simple and effective bit of gear and every truck carried a pair. On the whole the desert was as hard as concrete but you did run into soft patches and then the only way to get out of these soft patches was by brute force The sand channels helped. They were lengths of heavy metal about ten foot long and wide enough to take a truck's tyre. They were shaped in section like a very shallow 'U' with a lip at the top . Get one of these under a bogged down wheel and you were away, for it was a well designed functional bit of equipment. I found out later that it was only because an officer had seen a huge dump of these back in the rear area and realised their possibilities that we had them at all. No doubt he too had had a tough time struggling to free his truck. The gear had been stock piled there since the 1914-18 war when they had been designed to be used as roofs over trenches.

Early in the January 42 we moved down from the desert in cattle trucks marked, 40 Hommes - 8 Chevaux . Lucky horses. I believe this marking was also something that survived from the 14-18 war. We moved again, this time to Syria. On our journey there, somewhere between Haifa and Acre, we saw an amazing and unexpected sight, cavalry. There must have been a few hundred of them on the shores of the Med and the object seemed to be that they went into the sea. All the horses were being ridden barebacked and the sunburnt riders hadn't a shirt between them. Both horses and riders merged in shades of brown so that they seemed almost as one. With the shouts of the exuberant riders and the whinnying and squealing of the excited horses it was a kaleidoscope of rearing, wheeling, kicking life and movement. It was like a time warp, for the cavalry of the ancient Greeks must have looked as they did.

But our view was fleeting. The convoy rolled on, there was no stopping. We passed the Dead Sea in the same casual throwaway manner. By coincidence a few days later and now in snow covered mountainous country we saw cavalry again, just as impressive but more restrained and controlled. These were Indians, bearded, turbaned, some with pennants fluttering from lances. They had mules with them carrying pack guns. We watched them for a time until the convoy moved on. The fighting with the Vichy French was over and our short sortie to Syria was akin to a move in chess to neutralise a threat to the Persian oil wells.

An operational nightmare for those in charge at this time was the fact that there simply weren't enough troops to go around for the tasks that needed to be done. There was a constant shuffling around of what troops there were on hand. At varying time demands in Greece, Crete, Syria, Persia and Iraq took away troops from the Western Desert always, as it seemed, at the most critical time. Our journey came to a halt near Homs and the platoon had an unusual billet. It had been a large work shop but what made it unusual was the supply of constant hot water from a hot spring just behind it and the fact that we had to go through deep snow to get at it. From here we were recalled. The Western Desert had greater need of us.

From about this time my life in the army changed. I was told to pack my kit and report to the Intelligence section or the "I' section as it was known. It was a change for the better in all respects, then because it was a much more interesting job and now with hindsight because I am probably still alive through it. The reason I was moved there was pretty straightforward. I had an aptitude for drawing and the maps became my job. I did wonder how they found out I could draw but now when I see the crude little sketches I illustrated my letters with, and as they were all censored by the platoon officer, I suppose it was obvious. We talked about the officers and I have no doubt they talked about us. So a conversation between Lieutenants Mills, who commanded 12 platoon and censored my letters, and Barnett, who was the Intelligence Officer, probably decided my life. The situation map was the map that mattered. The map would be of the area the battalion was in and on its covering of talc, as it was then called, friend and foe would be crayoned in, the opposition in black and ourselves in red. The names of the opposition soon became familiar to me, the 21 st Panzer, the 60th Light, the Ariete, the Trento, the Littorio etc. I became a man with information.

Besides the change in my duties the role of the battalion was changed. It became part of the Support Group of the 22nd Armoured Division which itself could be split up into three sub groups. Whichever way it was composed it was considered to be a mobile, fortified strong point out of which armour could operate and retire to. 'Boxes designed to form pivots of manoeuvre for the mobile armour' was the technical phrase used. As part of this reorganisation our C.O. was given the command of the Support Group and as he moved to Brigade HQ and took the Intelligence officer with him, and the Intelligence officer took me, I lost contact with 12 Platoon of Z Company.

At the time of this change we were stationed more or less a stone's throw from the Pyramids and the Sphinx. As Napoleon told his troops on the eve of a battle when they were in this area, "From the summit of these pyramids, forty centuries look down on you". I must shamefully confess though they looked down on me too and I looked across at them I never got around to visiting them. I doubt if many others did. Probably they thought as I did: they've been there a long time now and they will be there a long time yet. Also one had to weigh up the attractions of the past of

Egypt with the present, represented by the pleasures of the Berka. The Berka, which was an area of brothels and bars which had catered for British troops for many years, won hands down.

Before we went back up the desert the names were called out of the LO.B.s. (left out of battle) - the men who would form the basis of the next battalion of Northumberlands if the present ones didn't survive . I was there when it was read out and there were some facetious comments - they were Jewish almost to a man, Solomoms, Abelson, Levi and so on. But through no conscious effort of theirs -they were the best men for the job they were doing, jobs which most of them had being doing in civvie street such as company tailor, barber, pay clerk, etc. But it raised a laugh.

The recognised method for troops to travel in the desert was in "boxes". The name box because that was approximately the shape of the area the vehicles covered. The principle was that the hard-skinned vehicles, armour, Bren carriers and artillery for instance, were on the outer edge of the box and the thin-skinned vehicles - mobile workshops, signal trucks, ambulances and suchlike - in the centre. But there was a place for everybody, Engineers, Ordnance, Quartermaster, Anti Aircraft etc. It needed over a thousand vehicles to move a Brigade and one of the memorable moments of my army career happened when I was alone in the Intelligence truck and a message came asking for the bearing that one would need to get to some specific map reference. I casually ran the bearing off, gave the course and then watched in amazement as vehicles as far as I could see started up into action. I had returned to the map to check my calculation when the Intelligence officer came haring back and did it for me. For a time I rode along looking at the familiar sight of the Box on the move with a sort of proud and proprietorial interest and thinking that it was all my doing. It was God like.

During daylight hours the vehicles travelled or parked well apart so that they did not provide too easy a target for enemy guns or aircraft and at night they closed up to make it easier to withstand attacks from infantry and armour. The enemy used the same method to a certain extent and with the hundreds of vehicles it made a huge target area. Any shells that arrived in it were at worst a near miss. The surface of the desert itself was in the main rock hard so that the shells did not bury themselves but exploded on the surface with flying rocks being added to the lethal outburst. Apart from the shells it was, in an odd way, like a mobile village, and you got to know where people "lived." Particularly in your own neighbourhood. Only the almost limitless space of the desert made it possible and the desert was, if you can have such a thing, an ideal battleground. It was said of it that it was a tactician's paradise and a quartermaster's nightmare. Over this desert travelled our "Box", our home.

In a letter I wrote home at the time: *We are up in the blue again and we have just got up in time for the warm weather. It is a queer life this with a 1 5cwt truck as your home. On our truck there is the RSM, an orderly corporal, the driver, the RSM's batman, another chap in my section and yours truly. We manage nicely as long as the rations and water come up regular, especially the water. All we do is wander about the desert picking up rations and water at prearranged points and on with our roaming. We shave about every three or four days and as long as the trucks and vehicles go and the guns fire no one bothers us. Bully and hard tack come up every meal, sweltering every day, freezing every night. Reveille is generally 5 o'clock and we move at 5.15, stop for breakfast about 9. But we manage. Was just thinking the other night how easily we settle down. It was just as the sun was setting and every one was closing up - we were bumping along, the RSM was on top of the cab to get the breeze, the driver driving with no shirt on and the windscreen up, the corporal sleeping, the other two were cleaning the Bren (we had been attacked by enemy aircraft) and I was dubbining my boots, while all around there were trucks, carriers and armoured cars as far as the eye could see. Everyone just going on as if they were in their back garden or some place like it at home.*"

Because of this structured method of travel we generally had a good idea of where everyone was, so when we suffered our first casualties I knew immediately that they were in our battalion. The attack was from the air and I watched the planes go down the line of trucks. Plumes of smoke went up as two trucks were hit and obviously somebody must have got the knock. The depressing thing it was so obviously a mistake as we could all see that the planes were Kittihawks. No one fired back and they were gone as suddenly as they had arrived. Later we received a letter of apologies from the South African squadron responsible. If there was time you could identify yourself by setting off coloured smoke canisters but there seldom was time. It was a fairly common occurrence in the desert where there were no fixed lines. Perhaps it evened itself out as I doubt if the German pilots were any better than ours and, as the Afrika Korp seemed to make more use of our captured vehicles than we did of theirs, the chances of mistakes on their side would be greater.

It was incidents like that that gave the 8th Army the name we always knew it by - The Mickey Mouse Club. In the news reports of the day it was always referred to as The Desert Rats from the Divisional sign of the 7th Armoured, which was of a jerboa with its connotations of being quick and sharp and at home in the desert. Later this came to be applied to the entire 8th Army. But I cannot recollect anyone in the desert referring to themselves as a Desert Rat. Some of the old hands who had been in Wavell's earlier battles would say with satisfaction that they had been with Wavell's Wankers but the name they gave to the 8th Army goes back further than that. In pre-war England every town that had an Odeon cinema had a Mickey Mouse Club. It was for children only and it must have been a godsend for parents on a Saturday morning. I should imagine everyone in the ranks had been a member at sometime. The Mickey Mouse Club is what I always heard the 8th Army called, or, to give it its full title, The Fucking Mickey Club. With incidents such as the Kittihawks shooting us up, it was putting it mildly, an understatement. I appreciate why the name Desert Rats appealed to and was used by the press. Ultimately instead of just the Divisional sign of the 7th Armoured Division it was applied to the entire 8th Army, and later Churchill was to write something to the effect that if in the future people asked you what you did in the war, it would be sufficient to say, 'I marched with the 8th Army.' I can see that 'I marched with the 8th Army' has got a far more resounding ring about it than 'I marched with the Fucking Mickey Mouse Club.' But that's the way it was.

The jobs I had to do now were far different and more interesting than when I had been in 12 Platoon. One job which I liked was to take the water trucks to be filled. It was Gunga Din on a large scale (about three hundred gallons a time). Water was a Number One priority in the desert and the water trucks were constantly on the go. The only drawback was that on the whole the water, because of the desalination that was necessary, tasted pretty horrible and although we were issued with tablets to make it palatable, a strong brew of tea with lashings of condensed milk and sugar was what was needed to kill the taste. And by some alchemy it turned it into a drink fit for the Gods. The army saying "When in doubt brew up" must have had its origins in such brews.

Sometimes the water point was close by, but other times it was considered that the drivers needed a navigator. This was supplied by the 'I' (Intelligence) section. In this, my first trip, I went to the rendezvous, saw that there was the correct number of water trucks, took a compass bearing and off I went, my little convoy following confidently behind. They little knew with what trepidation I led the way. As a back up to the compass we had a sun compass which worked roughly on the principle of a sun dial, using the shadow of an upright metal pin in conjunction with Greenwich mean time. The great point about the sun compass was that it was unaffected by the magnetism of the vehicles and it worked if the sun shone, which it generally did.

As I have said, a job I liked but as luck would have it I didn't get a lot of it. Travelling across the desert was like travelling at sea. It was flat and pretty near featureless and it could be tricky, but if you had a landmark or two - a knocked-out tank, a crashed plane or a grave - the job would be easy. It paid to notice at what angle you passed these landmarks for the return trip. There was always an eager reception party awaiting our return and it was nice to feel wanted, although the temperature, somewhere in the region of 100 degrees F, and metal too hot to touch and and having an empty water bottle might have had something to do with it.

Shellfire was a fact of life with good days and bad days and I will always remember the first time I was under serious shellfire. I had, in a manner of speaking, beginner's luck. I was walking past a truck alongside of which four or five Indians were standing. There were quite a few shells landing in the area but this one was obviously going to land close. Commonsense should have told me to hit the deck, but I had been brought up on the standards of boys' magazines such as the Hotspur, The Wizard and the Rover and the books of Biggles and Bulldog Drummond and Kipling, where Britons were a superior race who set the standards and all coloured people were "lesser breeds" The Indians, probably veterans of the Eritrean campaigns and Wavell's early affairs in the desert who knew what carnage and slaughter a shell could cause, had no such inhibitions and went down as one. I walked on and luckily I was unscathed, but this was a habit I speedily got out of. After all, the object of shellfire was to kill you and it was a bit pointless to help the Germans in their war efforts. It caused most of the casualties as it was.

Although one soon got to be able to judge where a shell would land and act accordingly, anyone who has ever been under sustained shell fire will never forget the feeling of concentrated viciousness and murderous power when a shell landed in the vicinity. And after you had seen what a shell could do to a man it needed a conscious effort of will to keep control of oneself. Shellfire became part of our normal life. A fair bit of my job was delivering messages and if they were relatively "local" and I had to walk it became second nature to keep an eye open for convenient slit trenches. A slit trench was a lifesaver in the true sense of the word.

A person I now came in contact with was the Commanding Officer, Lt.Col de Graz. A regular soldier who had come to the Northumberlands from the Rifle Brigade, he was tall and lean and always wore the old style riding breeches, tight at the knee and flared out at the side and which flapped as he stalked over the desert. His slightly bandy legs accentuated this and earned him the nickname of Flappy. He had one foible which one had to remember - he had a small cigarette case which he had filled every morning with three Turkish cigarettes. He smoked one of these after every meal and there was no doubt about it - he didn't like being interrupted when he was smoking them. For a time when he first took over the Battalion he was not at all popular. This was because he still retained a Rifle Brigade cap badge. But he knew what he was doing. He retained his old badge until the first action we had under his command. Things went well in this affair and the day after he started wearing a Northumberland's badge. Nothing was said but everyone got the message. Nowadays they would call it applied psychology or man management. But whatever it was it improved his ratings.

There were times when I had to go, like Mary's little lamb, with the C.O. to carry his map. Sometimes it was to conferences, going inwards in the box, but at other times we went the other way out when he wanted to have a look around. Wherever he was he always acted as if he was bomb proof. One day he went to look at some old positions to see what was left of them and if they could be utilised. We were standing on a  slight rise, he studying the ground with his binoculars and myself with his map, when we attracted the attention of some German gunners. They sent a few shells over but fortunately missed. However when they missed they generally learned from their mistakes and they started to improve. On this occasion the improvement was quite rapid and I thought the C.O. was pushing his - and by the nature of the job - my luck. I know his driver, Fidler, had the engine running when he leisurely returned to his car, which had been sheltering behind the ridge. It was probably doing its maximum speed by the time the C.O. had closed his door. I had already vaulted into the back.

Naturally officers, especially commanding officers, had to act like this but just as obviously it was stupid. All that training, experience and education just waiting to be knocked out because it was considered to be the done thing. The top brass also thought this and tried to do something about it in a small way. To show their contempt for shellfire most officers wore their soft hats, and it came on orders that all officers were to wear their steel helmets. This was done for a bit but we received some news that put it all back to square one. It had happened at some conference for commanding officers. The meeting was going on, the C.O.s in the centre with their drivers, underlings, trucks and cars dispersed around them and all of them wearing steel helmets. What took their minds off the job in hand was that there was a good breeze blowing and somebody's steel hat blew off and went rolling along the desert. It was made from cardboard. When covered with the regulation camouflage sacking it was indistinguishable from the real thing, unless of course if it was hit by a lump of shrapnel.

Nevertheless everyone was most impressed and probably regretted that they hadn't thought of it first themselves.

Although I did my Mary's little lamb act with the C.O.'s map, when he went on conferences and recces my main job was map work. There was plenty of scope as the maps were pretty near blank with only a grid line of ten mile squares across them. Sometimes on the desert itself, at the point where the grid lines crossed, there would be a cairn or an oil drum filled with concrete and a number which had either been written in the concrete before it set or painted on the drum. There could be nothing else for miles. I layered maps, with just a few feet between contour lines, and kept the situation map up to date. Because of this I knew who our neighbours were. Once when word ran around that some one had seen a woman driving a staff car I surmised, incorrectly as it turned out, that she was French, as I knew the Free French were south of us at Bir Hacheim (now known for being a station on the Paris metro). The woman, whom I never saw, the only woman amongst thousands of men, I have since found out, was English, and the only woman to serve with the French Foreign Legion . She is always brought to mind when I come across the word 'frisson' in a book. The other interest with being in the "I" section was the amount of information that came in to it. Some of it was quite intriguing. One bit that I would still like to know the full details of was a report from a patrol that picked up a man who was stark naked. As he wouldn't speak they did not know what nationality he was. We received the Germans' league table of their opponents, in which we found out that the New Zealanders were the troops they least liked to meet. They also coveted the well sprung 15cwt Morris wireless truck and any that were taken had to be sent to their rear echelons immediately. The information flowed in constantly.

The interrogation of prisoners was a job that was done at the "I" section by the Sergeant, Webber. There was one thing I could never understand about the Italian prisoners - all of them seemed to have a collection of dog-eared pictures of sacred subjects, madonnas, crucifixions, various saints etc. and invariably a good number of them would have another collection in an even more dog-eared condition of 'feelthy postcards'. I used to shuffle them together before I handed them back, but I think the sarcasm was lost on them. One truculent German had a photograph of a group of cyclists taken outside a Derbyshire Youth Hostel which I recognised, an unexpected reminder of home.

Later I came across some photographs in what had been a German company office that brought home to me the difference in national character. They were all of war graves, technically perfect, pin sharp, ready for posting to the next of kin of the names shown on the standard issue of German army crosses, Soldiers for the Use of. What I found odd was what was in the background of these photographs. Almost in every case there was a truck loaded with bodies. The fatigue party who had got this job were shown standing on the corpses as they unloaded their macabre load. I couldn't help but think that they were a bit insensitive to send photographs such as these to the next of kin of the deceased. However they did send them whereas all the British sent was an official card.

Another time when swanning around in the blue we came across what had been a German quartermaster's store and I found a box of cut throat razors. They were all marked Soligen and had gold inlaid bone handles. As my father still used a cut throat razor for shaving I sent him one. I kept a couple for sharpening my pencils and a couple I put on one side for trading with when I went on leave. Most of the platoon got at least one and the majority of us did try at least one shave with them. The following morning the end result could be summed up in one word: bloody.

There was a lot of trading done in this manner, the only drawback being that the standard of living of the Egyptians was so low that they could never afford to pay you much. The other thing I got from that store was the last thing one would expect in the middle of the desert, a bath. It was a memorable bath. Among the gear that littered the place was an oil drum half full of fresh if slightly rusty water. Someone saw the possibilities and we jacked it up and heated it up a little. To do this we used the time-honoured but wasteful method of the early 'Desert Rats' in the pre Tommy Stove days. We filled a cut down petrol tin with sand, poured petrol into the sand, then put a match to it and pushed it underneath the oil drum. We cut cards as to what order we went in. It was luxury of the first order. In the midst of a world that was dry, arid, harsh and with water at a premium, it was approaching decadence, way beyond asses' milk, to stand in luke warm water, probably the equivalent of a Company's supply for a day, to cover oneself in lather and then sink, kneeling down in the water - it was to experience something almost beyond our memories.

It was my turn to indulge in this sybaric manner when some Stukas arrived in the area. Common sense told me to join the others in the old German slit trenches but I just couldn't bring myself to do it. Soap suds and sand? Never! There were lots of other targets. Someone gave me my tin hat. I stuck it on and stuck it out and fortune favoured the clean.

CHAPTER 6

Leave after a spell up the desert was a marvellous experience to wake up at your leisure between clean sheets, in the first bed you had slept in since leaving England, with the sun streaming through the open window and lie, blissfully aware that the day was your own far from the range of shells, the realm of Company Orders or beyond the reach of the Orderly Sergeant. A call to a "Gyppo" servant - there was one on every floor - and he would bring you a pot of tea and over it you would leisurely plan your day.

My leave had mixed attractions. I saw 'Gone With the Wind' in Cairo. The screen had three panels, one below and one on each side of the screen, carrying translations in Arabic, French and Greek and all flickering disconcertingly, sometimes one panel full of characters and the other two almost blank. It made one wonder about translators. Most of the cinema audiences would be British troops and in those days cinemas always ended with the National anthems, here both British and Egyptian, to which all would stand. If that had been all, all would have been well, but the troops always bawled out the bowderlised version of the Egyptian National anthem. It started:

"King Farouk, King Farouk,
Caught his bollocks on a hook
King of the bints (women) and the dogs,
And the beggars and the wogs. . . "

and it went on getting steadily more obscene. I can now imagine what the Egyptians, who generally spoke English, thought of us.

I went to an art exhibition and lecture by a war artist - I think his name was McIntyre. There was one painting of a New Zealand gun team at Sidi Rezegh and it brought to mind that some one who had been at Sidi Rezegh had told me about a New Zealand gun team he had seen there, "Like a tableau at Madam Tussards" - all at their positions and unmarked, but dead. It was put down to blast. A shell had landed close and though it hadn't hit them it had killed them as it had blown their lungs in and then sucked them out. He went on in his lecture to talk about the problems he had with the hard straight line of the desert horizon that divided all of his compositions. I appreciated what he meant but thought that there were a lot of people up the blue who would have willingly swopped their problems for his.

Cairo in those days was seething with troops and it was by sheer chance in my wanderings that I met another Northumberland Fusilier with whom I had done my training at Fenham Barracks. We had a drink together and talked shop. He had left Fenham a couple of drafts before me and gone on to the 1st Battalion in Tobruk. He had recently been on a shoot which had gone like the exercises we had done at Fenham except for the ending. It had been noticed that the Germans in their area had occasionally been using a desert track, so four guns had been sent out one day to see if they would be lucky. They had set up their guns behind a small ridge on fixed lines, which meant that after the range had been worked out the guns were clamped on that range to hit a specific area on the track. After that they simply had to wait until the target arrived at that point and fire the guns. It was their lucky day for, after a couple of hours wait, six trucks appeared led by, they assumed, an officer in a 'people's car', the fore- runner of the Volkswagen. It was all over in seconds, two trucks on fire, the rest useless and, through the glasses, it appeared that their occupants were all satisfactorarily dead.

Ten minutes later, with the gunners relaxed and the guns still clamped and no one behind them, the People's Car started up and, before they could do anything about it, disappeared in a cloud of dust. They worked it out that the driver had had the imagination to stop immediately he had come under fire on the assumption that once he stopped he would no longer be considered a target, then a ten minute wait to allow everyone to relax and then he had put his foot down and got away. My companion remembered his Sergeant's anger and his remark, "Them's the bastards that shouldn't get away, the clever ones". I also discovered why Vickers machine gunners were about the only troops in the desert that never wore shorts. It was for the obvious reason that the empty cartridge cases fell into the legs and they were hot. He also told me that of the draft that had left before mine to join the 1 st Battalion, two of them had got the knock within the first three hours of arriving in Tobruk. I worked it out that if I hadn't gone on the NCOs' course I would have been on that draft. The Northumberlands motto "Where the Fates Call" could be pretty apt, either way.

It was on this leave I also saw my first Americans. They had come over with the first American tanks, the long awaited Grants, and they were noticeable among the thousands of troops that were thronging through the narrow streets because they, non combatants among combatants, were all wearing a couple of rows of colourful medal ribbons. And as they were in cavalry units - cowboy boots with high heels!

I also made a point of visiting one of the local drinking places - I even thought I might see original belly dancers. It was cool inside and I was the only foreigner there among quiet Egyptian civilians who were all wearing a fez, drinking tiny cups of black coffee and smoking hookahs. They were listening to the wailing, or so it seemed to me, of a huge fat woman who was covered from top to toe in black and who swayed gently from side to side as she wailed. Disappointed and my curiosity satisfied, I left. I preferred the slim belly dancers I was accustomed to in the bars of the Berka, even if they did come from Bradford, Cardiff and such places.

The Berka was where most leaves were spent, an area of narrow streets where the traditional attractions of troops on leave, brothels and bars, predominated. The brothels never had any attraction for me but out of curiosity I did visit the ornate but seedy ante rooms of some of them. In one I saw an Aussie, big even by Aussie standards, who had taken a fancy to one particular girl. Unfortunately for some reason she did not take a fancy to him and was trying to put him off. His method to try and make her change her mind was to hold her by the ankles and dangle her out of the window, shouting at the same time "Will you or won't you, you black bitch!" As this was happening on the third floor she quickly succumbed to his blandishments. Considering what they did for the Axis' cause some of these girls should have been awarded the Iron Cross, as it was said that between them they put more men out of action through venereal disease than the Afrika Corp, and if not permanently it was constant.

On the last day of my leave I drank with three Australians from the 2/13 who were friendly because of my Northumberland cap badge. Although the siege of Tobruk is always associated with the Australians, they only provided the infantry. Everyone else - gunners, signallers, engineers, machine-gunners, etc. etc. - were British. The machine gunners in Tobruk were the 1 st Battalion of the Northumberland Fusiliers so my cap badge was familiar to them. The Australians were on their way back home because a Labour Government had just been elected in Australia and one of their election promises had been they would bring their troops home. On this last binge my leave was almost over and I was on my way back to the barracks when I was sidetracked into watching one of the side shows with which Cairo abounded. The main player was a Jock. Early in the day he had tried to check in his rifle as he was expected to do, but for some reason this hadn't happened. "It's nae fault o' ma ain," he told his appreciative audience. Now well into the evening with plenty of drink inside him, he was backed into a corner, his rifle with its bayonet now fixed and he with no intention of parting with it. The other players in this drama were four incensed but wary Military Policemen who were attempting to effect this parting. The audience were behind the Jock to a man, though giving the M.P.s plenty of dubious advice and encouragement. "Go in and get him, Corp! Now's your chance!" It finished when the Jock leant back against the wall, closed his eyes and slid to the ground dead drunk.

There were three Aussies near me. One glanced over and I'm sure the cap badge decided him. "Having a drink, mate?" And I went AWOL. From then on it was one bar after another. The bars that catered for the troops were a world apart from the one I had had coffee in. They were crowded and at some time or another sprawled at the tables and standing crowded at the long bars were men from every branch of every arm of the desert army. Most had a few months' pay to spend; all knew that life was fleeting and none of them gave a damn for tomorrow. Their attitude was covered in the phrase, 'Eat, drink and be merry for tomorrow we may die.' And for the moment the accent was on drink and as the evening wore on, on the songs and, later, brawls. There was the usual Nelly Dean and Kevin Barry, the Irish Rebel, a good tune but probably more popular because it was forbidden. Another favourite, a thumpy sort of tune, was the Egyptian national anthem. As I have said, now well and truly bowderlised. The mixture of English and Egyptian words had been put together quite well but as to the content, bawdy is putting it mildly. The South Africans had Sarie Marais but they also had a couple of Zulu war chants to which they used to stamp their feet in unison and which were pretty impressive. The Aussie equivalent of Nelly Dean was another popular one. It was about Gallipoli and told the story of a brokenhearted nurse "who beneath a Cross of Red swore to do her duty to her lover who lay dead." He on his part "had played his part that August day, And left her heart on Suvla Bay." I have seen hard bitten Aussies, "The Rats of Tobruk" as Rommel called them insultingly and which they took as a compliment, crying their eyes out as they sang it.

In the last bar we went into, The Sweet Melody, three seemingly boneless young Arab acrobats were performing incredible feats of balance on a tiny raised platform in the centre of the melee. They had barely finished their act when three drunken gunners attempted to emulate them. The crowd rose to this trio as a man and about a dozen went to assist them. These assistants, by standing on tables, managed to get this teetering trio upright on each others' shoulders but, although they had plenty of assistance to get up, once up they were on their own. When support was withdrawn, the inevitable happened. The collapse was spectacular and the top man was carried away unconscious. This act was much appreciated and appreciation was shown in the accepted manner, with coins showering down on the tiny stage. The three young Arabs who had been watching in the wings saw to it they didn't stay there.

By now there was broken glass under foot, the bar girls had disappeared and the band, who could read the signs, had let go of their instruments which were attached to wires that pulled them up to the safety of the ceiling. The entry of a Ghari horse which had been unharnessed and brought in by some New Zealanders who thought it needed a drink (they couldn't get the Ghari in as well) was the beginning of the end. The M.P.s were close behind.

Some New Zealanders had managed to get over the bar before the shutters went down and handed out every bottle they could lay their hands on so we left with the Aussies using their slouch hats like shopping baskets and myself with the top half of my battle dress stuffed with bottles. We ended up in the Australian Tin Hat club. Fortunately for me there was a spare bed in the room they had and it was here I awoke to find the room full of smoke. One of the diggers had gone to sleep with a cigarette in his mouth and set his blankets on fire. In my bemused state I saw him naked as the day he was born bundle up his bedding, but just before he flung it out of the open window he received the entire contents of a fire bucket wielded by a gyppo servant over his bare body.

These servants were on every floor and probably for the very reason I had just seen. This one was unlucky because after the digger had got rid of his burning bedding he ungratefully vent his annoyance on the servant. I heard him cry "You black bastard!" and heard the noise of someone been thrown unceremoniously down the stairs before my eyes closed again. When I awoke the following morning the Aussie was asleep on the wire mesh that had supported the mattress. He was a terrible sight as his body was criss crossed with weals caused by the wires cutting into his flesh as he had moved during the night but he was still asleep and snoring. In a letter I wrote I say, *"... woke the following morning to the sound of a barrel organ playing in the square below and from the balcony of the room, which is four stories high I could look down on the square with a fountain splashing in the middle and the green tops of trees which are spaced along the pavement, just how I imagine it to be in France. While along the sidewalks business men of every nationality bustle along on their way to work with their red fezs showing through the foliage. There was the clatter of trams and the sound of the small trumpet affairs the conductors carry in place of whistles intermingled with the blaring of klaxons. These chaps only use two things to drive with, accelerator and horn. On the whole a lively scene which I found pleasure in watching as I sipped a cup of tea one of the native servants had brought up. After that a bath downstairs, to the barber's for a shave, breakfast of bacon and eggs, and no queuing for it, said so long to the Aussies and returned to barracks."*

As always it was a letter for home consumption but I have no doubt my Father guessed there would be another side to it. All the letters I ever wrote home from abroad were censored but obviously I censored them first.

I was only a day late in reporting back so I received the normal sentence of so many days confined to barracks. As one was sent back to one's battalion to serve this, it actually meant confined to the desert, so life went on as normal. I was told of a regular gunner who killed an Egyptian and got the same sentence. The story I was told was that his Greek wife (in pre-war Egypt gunners could afford to be married) had complained that this Egyptian had been pestering her and hanging around their flat and one evening as he was returning with a few drinks inside him they had met. Unfortunately for the Egyptian some of the desert Army had got in the habit of carrying Italian bayonets They were quite short and as broad as sheath knives and with this he had killed him. What had turned this incident into something bizarre had been that somehow or other he had managed to hack the unfortunate Egyptian's head off and he reported back to barracks where he had deposited his grisly burden on the well scrubbed guard room table.

We left for the desert for the last time on the 23rd of April with the traditional red rose of St George, who was on our cap badge, stuck in the camouflage sacking of our helmets, and full of confidence. We were confident because of the arrival of the Grants. Though they were an obsolete American tank it was hoped they would help redress the balance with the German Panzers. At some time on the journey up my officer handed over his glasses and, pointing to some trucks, asked me to give my opinion of them. It was a fair time before I worked out that they were tanks which had been made to look like trucks. They were Grant tanks with a metal frame-work over them over which was stretched a canvas sheeting painted with the normal desert camouflage. The Grants were considered obsolescent by the Americans but were a godsend to the British. Until then the armour of the Afrika Corp had been more than a match for the Valentines, Matildas and Crusaders of the British which they totally outclassed, being faster, with a bigger gun and having thicker armour. The Matilda was known as an "I" tank, "I" for infantry. It was well armoured, but was designed to keep up with Infantry as they advanced in the 1914-18 war style, with a top speed of eight miles an hour. British tank design started with the limitation of what could be carried on the British rail system and the width of the railway tunnels whereas the Germans had designed their tanks and then the road transporters to carry them. These transporters were used by them in the field and often followed the panzers into action where they were used to recover damaged German and British tanks which could be repaired to fight again, whereas even a slightly damaged British tank was a total loss to us. Though more than welcome the American Grants had serious drawbacks, their use of high octane fuel being one of them, so when they were hit they went up like an incinerator. The Germans name for the Grants as Tommy Cookers was only too true. The phrase for a tank being hit, 'brewed up' was an apt if macabre description of the occupational hazards of tank crews and was generally considered to be the reason why tank crews were issued with revolvers, so they could shoot themselves, a more preferable death to burning. Another drawback of the Grant was that the gun it carried, though 75mm and with a much greater hitting power than anything we had had previously, was fitted in a sponson which had a limited traverse so that at times the entire tank had often to be turned to lay the target. This meant it could not be used in a hull down position and its height, for it was a tall tank, compounded this drawback. The other thing that would have made a difference was that the long promised 6 pounder anti-tank gun, though designed in 1938, hadn't arrived in any quantity. This would have gone a long way to redressing the balance with the German 88mm which was without a doubt the gun of the desert, or even the war. Nevertheless the arrival of the Grant was a very encouraging trend. Once it had been trucks camouflaged to look like tanks, not tanks to look like trucks.

Life in the desert was pretty basic. Your home was your truck. Normally these were 15cwt Bedfords, a model where your feet had to go straight out before you reached the pedals. In normal conditions this was a pretty comfortable truck to drive. but these were not normal conditions and if you ran over a mine the only protection for your behind and all that went with it was the thin sheet of metal that made up the floor of the cab and the seat cushion. To try and make up for this lack of protection in such a sensitive area, sand bags were laid on the floor of the driving cab. It made it uncomfortable and awkward to drive but everyone used them. The thought of running over a mine and shrapnel being blasted up your behind seemed worse than shrapnel anywhere else.

Whenever you stopped you dug a slit trench for yourself. It paid to dig one, no matter how short a time you thought you were going to stay there. Statistics proved (we got all this type of information in the Intelligence section) that the Guards who had much stricter discipline -they always dug slit trenches, irrespective - had less casualties than any other unit. Though once you had seen what an exploding shell could do you did not need much prompting, it became second nature. You did a lot of digging in the desert, in fact you generally started the day with a little digging. For bodily functions you took a spade and walked a little distance away from the truck and dug a hole, squatted over it and filled it in when you had finished. It was the accepted thing. We lost a man doing this during a sandstorm. He walked away from his truck and never found his way back. This basic rule of hygiene was strictly adhered to by both the Germans ("Der Spatengang", the walk with the spade) and the British, but not by the Italians, and you could tell their old positions by the flies. I believe they suffered accordingly with dysentery. Desert sores were another self explanatory problem but these were something every army suffered from.

At night you slept by the truck and it could be bitterly cold. The difference behind day and night was remarkable. You would be shirtless during the day but we often woke up with frost on our blankets and we would often be wearing our great coats up till about nine o'clock in the morning. For myself I generally slept underneath or close alongside the truck on a German stretcher I had found. This had the advantage of saving me from one hazard of the desert, which was being run over by vehicles that were moving at night. I heard it said that there were more casualties in the desert caused by vehicles than by the enemy. It happened on both sides, as I later read, an adjutant of Rommel's was killed in this way. It could be true when one considered that battles only lasted a short time but the traffic was constant and obviously lights were never used.

Food rations were generally tinned and were issued by the truck. And the system on most trucks was that the other ranks ran a cooking roster. One time we even had an issue of oranges, but by the time they reached us on their journey from depot we had to cut cards for them as they worked out at one between three! Nobody stole the bully beef and hard tack biscuits which came up time after time after time and whatever you ate there would be sand in it. I've heard men say, just as they would of salt, "It needs a bit more sand in it," and, bending down, they would take a pinch of sand and sprinkle it in their bully stew. It wouldn't make any noticeable difference. One could sometimes trade bully for eggs with the occasional Arabs we met, but only the Hereford brand. The reason for this preference was that it had a bull's head on the label and, as far as they were concerned, this was proof of its contents. The Germans and the Italians had their equivalent which we came across at times. The Germans called their tinned meat "Alte Mann", old man.

But there was one meal I had in the desert that was more than a little special. The sergeant who came up with the rations that particular night was the one with whom I had fallen foul in the past. He was of a nervous disposition, you soon found out who was, and he was in a hurry to get away, and our truck was his last call. But I held him up by vacillating. It was my turn to cook and what was on offer was the normal tins of bully or a large piece of meat. It was large because no one else had wanted it and it wasn't difficult to see why. When one shone a flashlight on it, it was for all the world like a huge lump of black rubber. As I hummed and hawed, the sergeant got more anxious than ever to be on his way, which I must admit, pleased me. He finally said I could have the entire piece of meat if I wanted it. I was tempted and, getting one of my cut throat razors, I made a cut in it. The inside looked as meat should, red and bloody. There were only four of us to cook for at that time so l could afford to waste some. When it came time to cook this hunk of meat I sliced off all the black outer layer and cut the rest into mouth-sized chunks and put it in the dixie with some tinned vegetables and left it on the Tommy Cooker while we got on with whatever was the job in hand.. What lifted it out of the ordinary was that, just as we were going to eat it, we got the order to move. The only thing I could do with the now cooked meal was to fasten the lid of the billy down and wrap it up in two or three blankets to keep it warm. About four hours later when we halted and were told we were there for the night, the bundle of blankets was carefully unwrapped and we opened the dixie. The aroma was what one would expect in a five star restaurant. As the aroma spread we could hear voices in the darkness commenting on it. We never even served it out. We simply put the dixie on the tail board of the truck and the four of us ate carefully and quietly, keeping our spoons from chinking on the sides of the dixie, and polished off what had been about twenty men's meat rations. It was a memorable meal. The four hours wrapped in blankets, hayboxing, had lifted what had been normal army rations into a gourmet experience.

There was one morning we had a good start to the day. I was shaving when I saw an ME 109 go zooming in on one of our Lysanders that was spotting. It was such a uneven contest that all who were morbidly watching assumed that in a matter of minutes the Lysander would be going down in flames. But the Lysander did the only thing it could do, dipped its nose and went flat out for the desert. The 109 confidently followed. Its pilot must have been so keen for the kill and, working on the assumption that if there's space for him there's space for me, he forgot the capabilities of the two planes. When it was almost at deck level the Lysander pilot put on his brakes and straightened out literally feet off the ground. The 109 went straight into it. It was fantastic. The Lysander climbed leisurely back up again. As I've said, a marvellous start to our day.

I was told of another ME 109 that came to a sticky end in an odd way. It was triggered off when a South African Brigadier, to motivate his anti aircraft gunners, promised a crate of whisky to the first gun team to bring an enemy plane down. The pilot of the plane that was brought down was being quite clever, but in an odd way he was hoisted by his own petard. The Western Desert was bounded both North and South by cliffs or escarpments and the German pilot was flying back to his base over the beach bordering the Med and on a level with the escarpment. He knew he was safe from any anti-aircraft gun on the desert itself as they couldn't be depressed low enough to fire at him. But he was seen by a South African Bren gunner who was on the lip of the escarpment and had just assembled his gun after cleaning it. When the ME 109 reached him it was exactly on his level and literally only yards away . He opened up and killed the pilot with his first burst. He claimed the reward and although it wasn't what the Brigadier had intended it was what he wanted. The promise was honoured and the case of drink was handed over with a good heart.

But sometimes things went the other way. I was going somewhere once with a message, now long forgotten, when someone asked me to give him a hand. He had just laid a blanket by the side of a man who was lying on his back smoking, and he wanted me to help him lift him on to the blanket and then into a truck. As far as I could see there was nothing wrong with the man, no wounds, no blood. I got hold of his ankles, lifted them and both his knees bent the wrong way and his legs came off in my hands. It was one of the greatest shocks I have ever received in my life. I put the legs down, and the now legless man kept on smoking. A sliver of shrapnel had done the damage.

Shortly after that I had a stroke of good luck. I was passing a troop of twenty five pounders who were hammering away; close behind them were the Quads, the trucks that towed the guns, and one of their drivers asked me if I wanted a cup of tea. The driver was sitting in a slit trench that ran alongside the quad. He had a standard issue Tommy Cooker going with a dixie of water boiling on it before him, and without hesitation I joined him in the trench on the other side of the Tommy Cooker. Tea was something you never seemed to be able to get enough of. The water boiled, the tea was made, poured out, condensed milk added, and then he asked me to get the sugar. "It's in a tin box on the floor of the Quad. Just open the door and you can reach it." He was quite right. I stood up in the trench, opened the door, got the sugar and sat down, and was just putting my hand up to close the door when a piece of shrapnel tore a hole through it as big as my fist. Three or four seconds earlier and it would have gone through me just as easily. As my host remarked, "That could put you off sugar for life."

Another time, drinking more tea, I was with some of my old platoon and I noticed one of them was sitting on a square stone covered in some odd looking hieroglyphics. On asking how it came about I was told it had been picked up near Baalbek at some excavations when we had been in Syria and had been on the truck ever since. They used it for breaking firewood. I have no doubt it confused some archeologist at some later date wherever it ended up. Another time I was chatting with some of my old Platoon about a rumour that some medals had arrived in the

Company Office and the memorable point was that the majority there agreed that if any medals were going one man should have one. It was not because he had done anything exceptionally brave but that he was the one man in the Company who had signed on to stay in the army as a regular soldier. It seemed a strange place to be discussing another man's future but the assembled company had no doubt a medal would be of more use to a man in the army than one in civvy street.

There was an evening shortly after when Fidler and myself had a couple of tanks too close for comfort. It was almost dusk when we heard the familiar rattling squeak of tanks approaching. There were two of them and they seemed to be coming directly at us and we assumed they were German. We were on foot but there was a slit trench nearby and we lost no time in occupying it. But had they seen us? Unless they had infantry with them, prisoners were an embarrassment to tanks - what could they do with them? They had two choices, let them go or shoot them. It was then that Fidler asked me what came after 'Our Father who art in heaven'. For some reason best known to myself I refused to tell him, arguing righteously that if he had left it as late as this to make peace with God he deserved all he got. While this theological discussion was taking place the tanks rattled nearer and it was apparent they were going to pass us a few yards to one side - and even more to the point they hadn't seen us. So as the tanks disappeared I told him what he wanted to know and we lived to pray another day.

Because of the ability of the British to read the Germans' code through Enigma, it was known that Rommel was going to attack in May and, as a minefield had been laid from the coast to a point forty miles south named Bir Hacheim, a strong point held by the Free French (mainly their Foreign Legion) and Poles, the British commanders knew the Axis forces would either have to break through the minefield or go south round it. Interspersed in this minefield were 'boxes' of Brigade strength. The 150th brigade was in one of the boxes. When Rommel attacked he went south of this defensive line, around the bottom of it, then swung North.

Confident in his usual tactics and in the superiority of his weapons, he was expecting a quick victory. Initially for Rommel all went well and one of the first British troops he encountered were a detachment of the 22nd Armoured Brigade Support Group who were dug in about three miles South of us and in which was my old "Z" company . They were far too weak to stop the full force of the Afrika Korp in flight and by the end of the day, the 27th of May, the box as a fighting unit had ceased to exist. Only a few managed to get away to the North and join the main body of the Support Group which itself was linked up with what was known as the Knightsbridge Box, occupied appropriately enough by the Guards' Brigade. Rommel continued his advance but the British now had some of the new Grant tanks and a few of the new Six pounder anti-tank guns had arrived and although there weren't enough of either there were sufficient enough to deny him a quick victory and the supplies he had planned on capturing.

For three days the battle went on with the British getting increasingly confident of success. Later Rommel's adjutant was to write, "For the first time we began to have doubts about the superiority of our weapons." A month later Rommel himself was to reiterate this in a report. "Time and time again in our favour is the fact that some German weapons were superior to their British counterparts especially with regards to armoured vehicles. In the new British tanks and anti tank weapons however it is already becoming apparent that a qualitive superiority is developing in some of the British weapons. It is clear that if this comes about it would be the downfall of the Afrika Korps".

Rommel was now in dire straights, with his long lines of communications stretching South of the British minefields. Running short of water, fuel, ammunition and reinforcements, he called off the engagement on the 30th of May. Initially he was thought to have retired, but in fact he withdrew to the British minefield and took up his positions there, an area that later became aptly known as the Cauldron. This position, a half circle with its back to the minefield, which prevented him being outflanked, also prevented him getting his desperately needed supplies through. There was a gap in the minefield to the North of his position which was held by the Brigade we had previously been with, the 150th, and on this brigade Rommel, after leaving a thin defensive line around his position, threw the full weight of the Afrika Korp. It was absolutely essential for him that they broke through here to allow his supplies and reinforcements to get to him before the British attacked. He led the attack himself and on the 1st of June the 150 Brigade, having ran out of ammunition fell to the Afrika Korp.

Later Winston Churchill was to write about this action: 'During the first week of June the battle was therefore focussed on these two points, Bir Hacheim and the bridgehead. Within the latter was the stubborn 150th Northumbrian Brigade. Rommel was in dire need of supplies and water. If the whole battle was not to be lost, he must eliminate the brigade so that his convoys might pass. It was set upon and destroyed.'

Rommel also wrote about it, 'Yard by yard the German-Italian units fought their way forward against the toughest British resistance imaginable. The British defence was conducted with considerable skill. As usual the British fought to the last round of ammunition." Bir Hacheim, which was held by the Free French, fell shortly afterwards. The majority of the forces that had been in Bir Hacheim managed to get away but some were captured and here Rommel got a bonus. Some of the troops there were in the French Foreign Legion and as a good proportion of them were German, they simply changed sides.

With his supplies replenished Rommel was able to return to the offensive - a decision, it is said, triggered off by a note of pessimism detected in a message by a British Commander which they had overheard on the wireless. For the next five days the Cauldron lived up to its name, with attack and counter attack. One of them was a bayonet charge which I saw. It was made by the 2nd Highland Light Infantry, and there was no dash or wild Highland yells. It was impressive only by the cold courage shown.

They were part of an Indian Brigade which is generally composed of one British and two Indian battalions, one of the

Baluchis and the other of the Rajpatans. Being in the "I" section we knew it was going to happen and we watched them through our glasses. They arrived in 30 cwt trucks, jumped out, formed into two lines, fixed bayonets and started walking forwards. Their objective was Bir El Tamar ridge about half a mile away and it seemed to take them hours to get there. All the time there were mortars dropping amongst them and men falling. We could just hear the wail of the pipes, which sounded faint and thin in the vastness of the surroundings. They achieved their objective but in the evening they were given the order to withdraw and some of our vehicles went to help bring them out. They told us the positions they had taken had been empty, the Germans had withdrawn and, with the range to an inch, their mortars had inflicted heavy casualties on them. The piper, by the name of McPhee, came back on the truck I drove and later that night he played a lament. I assume it was The Flowers of the Forest and I doubt if any instrument but the pipes could have come anywhere near doing justice to the occasion. I suppose he was only doing what is laid down in Army Rules and Regulations but, following the rule book or not, I will never forget the emotions expressed by those pipes on that desert night so long ago.

Fifty six years later a neighbour, knowing I had been in the Western Desert, passed me a copy of the the Daily Telegraph saying "This obituary might be of interest to you". It was of the Medical Officer of the 2nd H.L.I. a Major Tilley and mentioned he had been awarded an immediate M C for his actions during the attack on the Bir El Tamar ridge.

Another attack I saw during this time was one put in by the Gloucestershire Hussars but I remember it mainly because of a million to one chance that happened at the time. There were two of us sitting on top of a truck watching the tanks as they went in at the charge, as was their wont. They always had to do this to try and get within range before it was worthwhile their firing. Except for the Grants all the British armour was out gunned. It was like two knights jousting but one had a lance half the length of his opponent. I still get reminded of this attack because one tank commander was blowing a hunting horn. He was probably blowing Gone Away and whenever I hear the sound of a hunting horn echoing over the winter fields at home today that action is brought vividly to mind. There was someone else in the area where we were but he was in a slit trench and just didn't want to know. To our reasoning we were quite safe. The only danger was from overshoots. Anti-tank shells don't explode. They are solid armour piercing shot designed to penetrate the tank then ricochet around inside, so any that miss their target simply bounce along the desert like cricket balls until they lose their momentum. To our reasoning the higher we were, the safer we were. It was because of our height we could see that the occupant in the slit trench was going to move; we could also see an overshoot bounding along in his direction and we both shouted a warning together. But it was to no avail. He popped his head up for a quick look at the exact moment the over shoot arrived, and it took his head straight off. If ever anything had a man's number on it, it was that anti-tank shell.

By an odd stroke of fate I received some mail at this time. A stick of bombs had fallen in our area and three of us on one side of a truck had been untouched but of the two on the other side one had been killed and the other slightly injured. He had been sent to the advanced dressing station, treated, kept for a couple of days and sent back. Just before he returned some mail arrived and he brought it back with him and I was one of the few that received it and actually read it. It included some photographs of my parents and sister, and for a few moments I was, in the midst of murder and mayhem, transported home.

Before this battle had started great hopes had been pinned on a new anti-tank gun which had been promised, a six pounder instead of the ineffectual two pounder. Unfortunately these guns never arrived in any numbers but we did get one or two. Both two pounders and six pounders were mounted on trucks, or portees, as they were called, and because of this and from a distance they looked somewhat alike. This gave rise to the death of one of the draft I had left the depot with. His name was Haddon and although not particularly friends, we had had an arrangement in our depot days over swapping rations. One day a week in those days we had been issued with field rations, part of which was one slice of bread and the rest hard biscuits. Because of his badly fitting false teeth Haddon couldn't manage the biscuits, whereas I could and had no particular preference, so we swopped - my bread for his biscuits. He was a quiet, inoffensive sort of person with thin, curly, grey hair which made him look prematurely old. But as we found he had a temper when pushed. There had been a tank attack in his area which had been repulsed and I was sent to collect what information I could for the regimental diary. I arrived in this part of the box and saw Haddon. He was dead but I couldn't help noticing that he had been shot in a strange way. The bullet had gone in under his chin and out at the top of his head. When I made inquiries I was told that when the German armour attacked, two of their Panzers had reached where we were standing. In the course of this action the six pounder on which Haddon had been serving had received a direct hit and most of the crew were knocked out. It was assumed that the tank commander in one of the German tanks had been curious enough and came to take a closer look at the new British gun. His tank was just drawing alongside the portee when Haddon recovered his senses and came to. It must have been one of the few times in his life when he lost his temper. Literally fighting mad, he had seized an empty shell case, stepped on to the German tank, grasped the officer by the throat and battered his brains out. A British officer who was in the area saw the possibilities, ran to the tank and threw his revolver up to him, with which Haddon leant into the tank and finished off the crew. Carried away with this success, he ran to the other tank and managed to scramble on to it but when he leant into its turret to repeat his act he was shot from below, the bullet going through his chin.

Another repulsed tank attack had a more acceptable ending. I was visiting one of the infantry platoons for some reason and there was an Mk iii in front of the platoon positions which had lost a track and someone in the area was convinced that the turret of it had moved. It turned out to be a fatal move. A couple of two pounder shots were put into it on the offchance and the tank crew, who had obviously been waiting for darkness to get back to their lines, were flushed out. But as every one who had a rifle was waiting they got no further. It was for occasions such as this we had spent our time on the firing ranges when at Fenham Barracks.

About this time I lost my officer Lieutenant Barnett. It was night time and some of our own tanks were returning to base, one of them running over the second Lieutenant. He had been sleeping in his valise over a slit trench but the valise was so bulky that when the tracks went over him it prevented him going deep enough into the trench where he would have been untouched. He called "Mike! Mike!" and when I first approached him he grasped my wrist for a few seconds with what seemed to me abnormal strength so that I thought he was uninjured. Then the strength went out of him. We assumed his ribs were crushed and the driver went off into the night to the Regimental Aid Post and I was left with him to do what I could, which was not much. He was having difficulty in breathing and couldn't see, but as long as he could hear my voice he was as composed as one could be in such a terrible situation. It seems such a simple thing to do, to talk, but I soon ran out of things to say. But immediately I stopped there would be a gasped, "Go on, go on." I was retelling him the story of "Frenchmans Creek" -which he had borrowed from the Adjutant and I had also been reading - when a truck arrived to take him to the advanced dressing station. I had often wondered if he made it back to his home in Worcester, but I met him again fifty-five years later. The Germans had patched him up and his sight had returned in an Italian PoW camp.

One who I know didn't make it was Brittain, a friend of my "Z" Company days, and with whom I used to swap books. It was early in the morning and I was on one of my trips to get information for the Regimental diary. I had got out of the truck and said to some one whom I recognised, "There's a fantastic smell of roast pork around here." "Yes," was the answer. "He does smell nice, doesn't he? It's Brittain." And he nodded to a burnt-out wireless truck. It was a black skeleton of a vehicle and sitting in what had been the wireless operator's seat was what looked like a small black shrivelled monkey, the remains of Brittain. The only good thing we could see in it was that he must have been killed immediately as he had obviously made no attempt to get out of the truck. There would be the ashes of a few Penguin paperbacks in there as well for someone - mother or girl friend, for he wasn't married - had kept him well supplied. What one needed in this place at that time was luck, and plenty of it, all along the line. Death became an accepted thing and taken for granted. To give an example, I was with a small group at one time when someone joined us saying, "Henderson has just got the knock".

" Which Henderson?"

" Henderson 72."

"I wonder who's got his lilo?"

Once three of us dived to the ground on hearing a shell arriving and the one of our trio who had dived beneath a truck and actually had his head against the tyre of the truck was hit in the head and killed. We lost an officer in a similar manner when he went to the other side of a truck to urinate. We survived and he was killed . As Kipling put it, "I was of delicate mind. I stepped aside for my needs."

On the fifth of June the powers that be decided that they wanted to get out of the engagement with as much as they could save to fight another day, and the armour of the 22nd Armoured Brigade was given orders to withdraw. The Support Group of the 22nd Armoured Brigade was ordered to stay and fight as a rear guard for as long as they could. Initially the frontal attacks were held but the Germans soon realised the weakness of the opposition and by late afternoon the box was almost surrounded. Ammunition had just about gone and by the fortune of war the last supplies that arrived were of petrol, at heaven knows what efforts of the drivers, who must have kept going West even when they must have seen that our armour was retreating East. They didn't get much of a welcome as nobody wanted them in their area when they did arrive, and shortly after their arrival I saw both the trucks go up in flames.

The situation map by now looked pretty depressing, the red bits shrinking and the black gradually surrounding them. I ended up as a rifleman in a slit trench and probably did as much good there as I ever did - after all I had been the seventh best shot out of my intake. At the end of the day the gunners said, in actions if not in words, "Have the fucking lot" fired the only ammunition they had left, which were smoke shells, and which must have told the Germans something, then went to sleep, exhausted. In some cases you couldn't tell the sleepers from the dead. Soon German tanks were among us. Everywhere there were burning vehicles with clouds of smoke rising from them and the constant crackle as the ammunition in them exploded in the flames. I was getting my water bottle and greatcoat out of the truck before I poured petrol over it and put a match to it when I saw the C.O. for the last time. There was a two pounder on a portee about a hundred yards away to my left with the gun team, Indians of the 9th Jats, standing alongside. Hurtling towards them was a Bren carrier in which the C.O. was standing erect, the only vehicle in the area that was moving, and it must have been travelling at its maximum speed with a dust cloud streaming out like a banner behind it. The fact that his was the only vehicle moving had already drawn attention to it and I have no doubt he knew what the end result would be and that he was consciously driving to his death. He jumped from the carrier as it reached the gun and ordered the gun team back on to the portee and climbed up with them. They managed to get two ineffectual shots off at the nearest Mk iii less than 100 yards away before they in their turn were hit by the Mk III's gun at pretty near point blank range. It was magnificent, stupid and the ultimate gesture - death before dishonour. But it was a pity about the Indians.

Almost at the same time as this happened another man also died because of pride, though another aspect of it. It was triggered off by a sergeant who took a calculated risk and made his point in a far more effective, though far less honourable, manner. In the midst of all this mayhem and confusion in the aftermath of battle with burning trucks and ammunition going off, there was one man who was exulting in it and living life to the full. I doubt if at that moment in time there was anything more that life could offer him. The epitome of the Aryan super race, a young blond Panzer officer, he was standing on top of his Mk iii and directing the prisoners that were straggling towards him. He was pride and arrogance personified. Today Africa . . tomorrow the world! The sergeant stopped by the slit trench I had been using about ten yards away from the truck. My rifle was by the side of it. He considered a little, then dropped his greatcoat and water bottle on the ground and dropped down into the slit trench. His hand came up and the rifle disappeared. He took a long time aiming but he didn't miss. I saw his target topple off the turret, his brief moment of glory over.

I threw a match into the back of the truck and as it burst alight flames shot up and the smoke billowed out, the sergeant emerged out of the slit trench, picked up his belongings, gave me a nod and continued on his way. With the truck now burning furiously I followed him through the smoke and joined the stragglers.

So it was that, on the 6th June 1942, the 4th Battalion Royal Northumberland Fusiliers (50th Recconnaisance Unit) ceased to exist as an effective unit. Of its original strength of 800 all ranks, there were enough remnants, L.O.B.s, men from hospital and the rear echelon, to make up a company of 4 officers and 106 men. Re-equipped with the new six pounder anti-tank guns, they fought a series of bitter rearguard actions in the retreat to Alamein. When they reached Alamein there were forty odd of them left. The Abington Mashers would go on the Mash no more.

CHAPTER 7

I had heard the phrase "For you the war is over, Tommy," two or three times but didn't believe it. I had met a few people who had escaped because we always had them at the "I" section for questioning to see what information they could pass on, and I had smugly thought, if they can do it so can I. But it didn't work out like that. I knew through having the job I had that we were already forty miles at least from our troops, and I was soon to find out that in the desert there was something that - more than having a minimum of guards - constrained the would-be escaper. It was water. Not everyone had brought, or even had the chance to bring, a full water bottle, so water was at a premium. The Germans themselves hadn't a lot, but at least they had the potential of getting some. I saw people draining the radiators of knocked out trucks and drinking the rusty red liquid they got from it.

Most of us slept from exhaustion that day and in the evening the moaning of a wounded man got too much for me and I went over to him. His wound wasn't bad, but he was only wearing a pair of shorts, and nights in the desert could be bitterly cold. I arrived at the same time as a sergeant in the the County of London Yeomanry. We decided that the best thing to do was to button our two greatcoats together and sleep on either side of him. The wounded man was lucky that the sergeant was in the C.L.Y. (County of London Yeomanry) – it was a territorial unit of the legal profession that had been mounted in pre-war days and his greatcoat had a very full skirt designed to go over the behind of a horse. (The Sergeant had been a solicitor and eight years later, by an amazing chance, he arranged the conveyancing of a house I bought).

In the morning the Germans collected our wounded and took them away on trucks and when we were ordered to move on I made my first attempt to escape. The snag was so did a number of others and we all used the same method. We laid in the bottom of a slit trench and got other prisoners to push sand over the top of us. The fault in the idea was that once one had been discovered every slit trench was checked. Two other prisoners who had attempted to escape were not so lucky. They had wriggled away undiscovered during the night and got a couple of hundred yards, probably far enough for them to think about walking, when they had both stepped on mines. They were lying in the mine field and still alive when we were moved on.

The Germans' method of feeding us was simple and basic. We were all lined up in rows, each row with the same number of men in it. A sergeant was put at the head of each row and given the food to distribute equally between the men in his row. After this had happened a few time there were some sergeants whom nobody would line up before, whereas the sergeant in the CLYs, Sergeant Thomson, had hundreds trying to get into the row before him. I do not say all the sergeants were unfair but, Tommy (Sergeant Thomson) was scrupulously fair. In fact if anyone went short it would be him. The fact that so many men singled him out was a genuine and unsolicited compliment that only he didn't seem to appreciate. He thought he was only doing what was expected of him.

We made our first acquaintance with barbed wire in a camp outside Tripoli. The food was basic, barely sufficient, and pretty soon few of us had energy to do anything except lie on the fine sand in the shade of the eucalyptus trees and doze. Even walking on the fine sand which slid from under your feet was an effort. I experienced a remarkable coincidence in this camp which I later wrote home about in a letter from Italy. I was lying in the sand idly sifting it through my fingers when a scrap of an English newspaper blew literally into my hand. I wrote, *"We were all in a bad way and more or less feeling sorry for ourselves, when a piece of newspaper about seven inches square blew on me as I laid on the sand. The scrap of paper was mainly taken up with a photograph and under the photo was a caption which read 'Kilshaw making his debut for Bury against Aston Villa'. That paper was over three years old and over 2000 miles from home and I stopped thinking about the flies and the heat and the hunger and the thirst and remembered when my Dad had taken me to see that match. One of the few football matches I ever went to see. It's an amazing world alright."*

83

I had become friendly with Tommy and he kept me and many others up to scratch. From somewhere or other he had got hold of a razor blade which he sharpened time and time again on a piece of glass he had found, so we were two of the few people that shaved, and that included the sentries. As he said, "We must keep up standards."

There was one book in the camp which we heard of long before we managed to get our hands on it and read it. It was an odd book in the circumstances, an account of climbing the Himalayan peak Nanda Devi with descriptions of snowfields, ice falls, blizzards and freezing temperatures whereas we were unable to walk on the sand with bare feet because it was so hot.

Evening was the best time of day when the sun had gone down and it was cooler. We could always hear the sound of children's voices from an Arab encampment that was close by. I thought then that kids' voices at play sound the same whatever the language, Italian, Arabic or Cypriot. Some evenings the off-duty sentries would sing. Distance may have lent enchantment but they were always worth listening to, with soloists and choruses and harmonies, and the tunes were generally familiar as they invariably sang tunes from operas. As some one said at the time, "If they could fight like they sing . . ."

Our time in Africa ended very quickly. There came a day when we were packed into trucks and in, it seemed, no time at all, we were on board a ship bound for Italy. It seemed as if our initial capturers had been correct and our war was over but, as it turned out, the phrase should have been qualified: it was only our war in Africa that was over.

Our guards for the voyage were happy and ebullient Italian troops going on leave. They were all wearing life jackets and the upper deck was packed with them, while the three cargo decks were even more packed with us. We were sprawled cheek by jowl on the iron decks. The cargo hatches had been left off so that some of us could see a square of blue sky above with Italian soldiers silhouetted against it. They were cock- ahoop and were calling down what we assumed to be Italian witticisms.

But their ribaldry came to a sudden end a few hours out when a klaxon started blasting away and, in an instant, the Italians were panic-stricken. We soon guessed why: it was a submarine alert. Whistles and bells joined the blaring klaxon amid the shouts and cries. But after the initial panic the first thing the Italians did was to batten down the hatches. We sat in darkness listening to the pandemonium above. To us it seemed as if every Italian on board was running up and down the deck above us shouting and screaming. All of us realised that if the worst happened we would go down like sardines in a can. We sat in the darkness, motionless and quiet. The idea of getting sunk by one of our own submarines seemed too ironic, yet fitted in perfectly with what could happen in the Mickey Mouse club. There were wisecracks to this effect and some of them raised a laugh. And I couldn't help remembering the first Italians I had seen wearing life belts the time they had drifted ashore and we had got the job of burying them.

But gradually things quietened down on deck and the panic was over. The hatches came off and we could see the sky again. The practice of allowing half a dozen men on deck at a time to use the latrines was renewed and we found a much subdued crowd of Italians. I like to think that the powers-that-be had worked out that the ship could have been carrying prisoners, and in fact that was the case, and few North going boats were attacked.

We landed at Naples. My first impression was how small the Italians were as a race and that the women who stood by the roadsides as we were marched away seemed sympathetic towards us. Perhaps they knew more than we did. Although we were now resigned to the thought of being prisoners, no one had any doubts but that we were on the winning side and I am sure that this showed.

Our first camp was a tented one at Capua, and some unfortunates suffered here from Italian inefficiency. We had been given various inoculations but records had been misplaced and some were inoculated twice, with the result that twenty six men died needlessly.

From here we were moved to a camp near Ancona. It was

here we had our first opportunity of writing home. We were issued with a form roughly the size of two standard post cards on which we could write. Having finished it and folded it together, you slipped a tag which was at one end into a slit and handed it in and hoped for the best. Mail had always been a highlight in the army but it became even more important in a prison camp.

The camp we were now in was composed of three large identical buildings, each one divided in half. We slept in three-tiered bunks and, as there was another one immediately alongside, it meant an area of 5'x6' held six men. These pairs of bunks were head to tail with another pair in a row of approximately twenty pairs of bunks. There was about an 18" gap and then another double row. They were too close together to walk between the rows. You had to go sideways. When you were on your bunk you could easily touch eight of your neighbours without effort. On intimate terms is the phrase that describes it. There were probably two thousand men in an area forty yards by forty yard. As only one wall had windows, there were some bottom bunks at the back where daylight never reached. Some were unlucky as regards

neighbours. There was one unfortunate who because of shellshock used to give a sort of yelp every five minutes or so. The ones in his vicinity often lost patience and hit him. The place was like a seething ant heap, but the accommodation didn't worry us too much as by now we could live anywhere. But the rations soon did.

In the morning we were issued with a cup of black coffee, made as rumour had it from acorns, and sugarless. Some time in the morning we received a bread roll, approximately as big as a man's fist, weighing 200 grams, and a finger of cheese. Later in the day we had about a pint of thin soup. This meagre diet started having an effect on people and fairly soon we had our first death.

The first funeral was quite memorable. A sergeant major, who was the senior British rank there, turned everyone out for a moving and impressive ceremony. But you can have too much of a good thing and on later occasions when he came into our section and shouted in his stentorian voice, "Outside to pay your last respects to a dead comrade!" he invariably got the reply, "Put him in the soup." At one time prisoners were dying at the rate of ten a week and although this was for various reasons the basic cause was starvation. Some one with a macabre and mathematical turn of mind worked out at what date the camp would be empty.

An anomaly amongst these walking skeletons were men who actually looked fat, but these were unfortunates who had contracted Beri Beri. Few people knew any thing about this disease except that it was thought to be a disease of the far East, but we found it was also known in Italy among the Italians and was due to a deficiency in their diet. In the main there were two general attitudes to this lack of food: one was to exercise as much as you could, which was simply a case of walking slowly around the exercise area, and the other one was simply to do nothing. Conserving your strength was the theory, and here we had what were called 'horiziontal champions'. They would get up for roll calls and food only, and some more or less went into a state of hibernation. Whatever theory we subscribed to we had only one subject of conversation and that was food. We thought about it and dreamed about it and everyone had their own fantasy concerning food. The greatest thing that life could have offered me at that time would have been a tin of condensed milk and a spoon. We had an ex-chef with us called Clark and sometimes we got him to talk us through a six course meal, from going to market to buy the ingredients, preparing them and finally to cooking them. It was pure masochism but we couldn't resist hearing a professional talking about food. We would sit around drooling and the request of "Give us a six course meal, Nobby," never palled.

We ran a roster, which was strictly adhered to, as to when each man's blanket would be used to collect the bread ration - the reason behind this was that some crumbs would be left in the blanket and a satisfying time could be spent gathering this windfall. There was one man in the area where I slept who did have an individual and potentially dangerous way of getting a little extra food. He was one of two French Foreign Legionnaires who had been captured at Bir Hacheim. He was a Swiss, a hairy barrel of a man and had once been a circus strong man. His method was to get up early every morning and be there when the small exercise area was opened up. This was an area that was bare, with the earth trodden down by many feet, but immediately surrounding it was a twelve foot border of grass stretching from the trip wire, which was a single strand of wire about a foot from the ground, to the barbed wire fence. Here he used to go looking for snails. The danger was in stretching too far over the trip wire. Go over it and you were considered to be making an attempt to escape and were liable to be shot. One man shot doing this was a Jewish sergeant, a very sincere socialist and an intellectual. He was killed in a manner of speaking by his good manners. Wanting to urinate, he stepped over the wire without thinking and was shot immediately. He was the second person I knew who was killed because of his finer feelings. The legionnaire had very little competition in his snail hunting. The other legionnaire came from Wigan and he told me he had joined the legion as a gesture, because he had come home early from night shift to find his wife in bed with another man. And another man who had left his home with a gesture of sorts had been a gunner in the R.H.A. or the Rocking Horse Artillery as

88

it was known. He came from Stafford and was the youngest of a family firm of painters and decorators. They had kept him working right up to the evening before he was due to report to the local barracks. On his last job he did something he had always wanted to do. He had painted the ceiling of a room gold and all the walls black. He had then shut the door on his work, hung up his overalls and gone to the wars.

What I thought was an odd sidelight on the Foreign Legionnaires was that both of them were expert knitters. They told me all legionnaires were and these two were constantly knitting socks with any bit of wool they could find. The Foreign Legion of those days, like the Italians who were guarding us, did not get issued with socks, only foot rags, squares of cloth with which they wrapped round their feet, so they knitted their own socks.

Our other problem, and it was no minor one, was the fact that we were lousy. Every one in the camp was infested with lice. These problems were inter-related, as healthy people are seldom lousy. It isn't people in dirty surroundings that become lousy, but those in poor and run down condition, and that certainly applied to us. Conversations often started with the number you had caught and killed that day. Getting out of your bunk and turning your blanket over had a certain vicious pleasure because you would always catch some of the pests scurrying for shelter. We were like monkeys, we picked them off each other as we talked and expected the same in return. One of the Italian Officers had a small pet dog which he sometimes brought into the camp with him and when someone bent down and patted it it invoked the remark, "Leave the little buggar alone, you'll make it lousy". On one of the delousing parades with which the Italians tried to alleviate this problem I saw Piper McPhee again. You had to parade with everything you had, bedding, clothes, etc. - anything that could harbour lice - and to the Italians this included the tartan covered windbag of his pipes. McPhee refused, protesting that it would ruin the leather of the wind bag - anything else but not his bagpipes. He must have won the argument because later I remember hearing him pipe in the New Year. Wherever you went in the camp you could always see someone with his shirt off going up the seams picking the lice out and cracking them between his thumbnails. If only they had been big enough to eat our two problems would have been solved.

In the midst of this there was one man who could see a positive side in our situation. He was called Bullard. In peacetime he had been an art teacher and he started running life classes. This was possible because we were issued with paper tokens with which we could trade for a very limited selection of poor quality articles. Pencils and exercise books were amongst this selection so we had the materials to work with. Also at this time we started getting a small and sporadic issue of cigarettes which immediately became the camp currency. Some men would even trade part of their meagre rations for them but it also meant that for a cigarette we could get an emaciated model to pose for hours. As Bullard philosophically told his pupils, and I was one, "You will get as fine a knowledge of bone construction here as anywhere else in the world." I remember talking to him in later days when the first Red Cross parcels had arrived . I had remarked on the beauty of the snow covered peaks of the distant Appenines. In reply he turned over an empty salmon tin and remarked on the marvellous translucent colours therein. The supply of paper which we could now get our hands on also allowed a pre-war journalist to start a wall newspaper, which gave me some interest as an outlet for drawings, cartoons mainly. It also had features on the jobs that men in the camp had previously done, a speedway rider and a jockey were two. As there seemed to be specialists in the camp on every subject under the sun, some very interesting articles resulted. News items were on such subjects such as the record number of lice one man had killed, the meeting times and places of various clubs and societies such as the Cycling Club, whose members met and talked of past runs, and lectures on subjects as varied as Welsh Culture, Socialism and The Advantages of the Louse. It also had an Obituary column. In fact it had everything a local newspaper has, and was also popular because of snippets of war news, provided in the main by one of the Italian medical orderlies who took the quite considerable risk because he was a fanatical communist.

Bullard could forget his surroundings as few others could and when he was doing sketches of a painting he hoped to do some day, it was of Jacob wrestling with the angels. He was in a world of his own. It was about this time that shit-house rumour had it that supplies of food had arrived from the Vatican. People who had contacts with the Italians, such as the medical orderlies, confirmed that some packing cases had arrived, and wishful thinking did the rest. Enough food to feed us for a month. Then came the word that a papal representative would be arriving to hand it over officially to the Sergeant Major. The camp was drooling at the mouth. Came the day, and there were packing cases all right, three of them, sent with the Papal blessing. But our dreams of gastronomatic delights were irretrievably dashed when the packing cases were opened and the contents revealed as six uneatable accordions.

After people had suggested where the Pope could stuff the accordions and had calmed down a little, it came out that a tiny minority in the camp thought that if not as good as they hoped it was not as bad as we thought. It seemed there were accordion players in the camp, and good ones at that. Accordions had been very popular instruments at that time, with accordion bands and national competitions for them. So a musical evening was arranged, which was bizarre. The performers were talented and keen but all lacking in one thing - strength. They were too weak to play. It was then suggested that there should be a completion for the best accordion player and the winner be put on extra rations so that he could entertain the camp. The competition was held and I doubt if any musical completion was played for higher stakes. The winner, the former amateur accordion champion of Great Britain, was installed as camp musician on an extra 200 grams of bread a day. But he soon handed in his notice. If the sound of an accordion could not be heard from dawn to dusk he was reckoned to be slacking, so the accordion joined the others back in the packing cases.

Although deaths were common, especially among the bigger men, (and some of the 'colonials' were big) there were two deaths at this time which weren't the norm. One man simply decided he had had enough and decided to die. There had never been so many doctors in the camp, he was such an interesting case, but their efforts were of no avail. He had decided to die and he gave up the ghost and died. The other death was even more unique considering the circumstances. Parcels from England had just started arriving. They were limited to ten pounds in weight and the few that had arrived contained socks, pullovers and suchlike but this man received a parcel par excellence, the one that every one wanted to receive. Nine and a half pounds of chocolate and a pair of socks. His mother must have had second sight to guess what he needed. The recipient had no particular friends to share it with and he was sensitive enough not to eat it in his bunk surrounded by starving men. Sometime in the small hours he went out to the latrines and that is where he was found. He died of an overloaded stomach. The general envious consensus was "What a marvellous way to die."

Shortly after we were all eating chocolate, not often but enough, as Red Cross food parcels started arriving. They were lifesavers in the true sense of the word and people who would have died lived. If we were lucky we would get one parcel each, but this was very unusual. Sometimes we received none for months, sometimes one between twenty men. This was the pattern for all British prisoners but there is no doubt about it, those parcels, erratic as their arrivals were, kept us alive. The effect on the camp when these parcels arrived was amazing, not only in the raising of the morale but in the noise generated. After the food was eaten the tins were left and this source of raw material released an absolute torrent of imaginative and creative work. Tin bashers was the descriptive name. The maker of a pendulum clock apologised, in a feature in the wall newspaper, because his clock lost about a minute a day, yet, except for a razor blade for its spring, it was made entirely out of empty tins. There were decorated trays utilising the different colours of the tins, lockers, suit cases, in fact tin bashing became so bad that ultimately it had to be restricted to specific times because of the noise. The reason for this was that more people wanted to sleep and all decisions were put to the vote in a democratic manner.

The Red Cross parcels coming into the camp caused another shortage, that of timber, or anything that could be burnt. A packet of tea was useless unless it could be brewed, a tin of stew was better heated up. In fact the parcels released another surge of creativity, cooking, only restrained by the lack of fuel. Every bit of wood that could be moved and burnt was moved and burnt. An example was one of the sentry boxes. This particular one was at the entrance to our compound and a group of frustrated cooks had waited patiently in the area until the sentry went into the guardroom for some reason or other. He was only gone a minute or so but it was enough. Every man knew his action station and they moved in. The sentry box left the area like a demented earwig. It turned into the first door and, running up to the three-tiered bunks, the snatch party dropped their booty and kept on running so that they wouldn't be brained by the rocks that were hurled down on it from above. In seconds the sentry box was match wood and every splinter had been picked up. By the time the sentry realised his loss it was as if it had never existed. The cooking fires smoked again.

The final solution to the fuel shortage was a technical one. By using empty tins the tin bashers constructed meticulously engineered burners, or 'blowers' as they came to be known. They worked by turning a handle linked to a system of geared up belt-driven wheels which turned a fan that produced a forced draught

Blowers Mk1   Mk2

that allowed previously unburnable material, the roots of trees, old boots, woven material, to burst into flames. Some of the later Mks of these 'blowers' were works of art. But then the tin bashers could devote a lot of time to them.

With the Red Cross parcels arriving people's horizons widened and as we got stronger we had the first escape from the camp. It may have been exceptional because the escaper could speak Italian, nevertheless it was imaginative, both in planning and in execution. When the guards were being changed in the camp the new sentries were led in by an Italian officer who strutted along with a string of sentries behind him. They went from post to post and watch tower to watch tower. The officer never looked behind and the sentries simply swopped over during the circuit. They then straggled out behind the officer through the main gate, put their rifles in a rack in the guard room and wandered off down the road to their barracks. It was this sloppy and undisciplined system of changing the guard that the escape was based on. Many of the men in the camp had been supplied with Italian uniforms because they had none of their own, so it was relatively easy to get a complete Italian uniform that fitted simply by swopping. The escaper then made a dummy rifle for himself, carving it out of bed boards which he stained with coffee. It was then quite simple to tag on to the end of the straggling line of sentries and make his way out with them. He had acquired some Italian money from somewhere, so he was able to travel by train and he was well on his way to Switzerland when he had the misfortune to go into an area that was out of bounds to troops.

Just at this period, as life in the camp changed for the better, twenty of us were sent to a work camp just outside Bolzano in the very North of Italy. Originally Austrian, it had been ceded to the Italians after the 1914-18 war and it was a German speaking area. The locals considered themselves Austrian not Italian and they looked like Austrians. On Sundays we would see them dressed up in their traditional costume, the women in colourful dirndl skirts and the men in lederhosen and Tirolean hats. Most of the people were bilingual and we found a lot of the local men who had been called up in the Italian army were serving in the Desert as interpreters with the Axis forces.

Ultimately this move to the North was to prove an unlucky one for us but at the time we thought otherwise. Mainly because the rations were better and we were away from the monotony and restrictions of the camp. The job we had to do was to build a tunnel which was to be a section of the Roma Berlin Strada. The work was not very onerous and our conscience was eased because we could see the war would be over before the tunnel would be.

Another plus point was that we were a very congenial bunch. It was here I first met Bob Warnock with whom I stayed to the end of the war. He was a regular gunner and had joined up when guns were horse drawn. He had been with pack mules in India and he could tell you tales that were pure Kipling. He had served with the 31 st Field Regiment in Eritrea before his regiment returned to the desert where he was captured. He had boxed for his regiment as a light heavyweight, billed as Bomber Warnock. Bomber was as easy as old boots up to a point, but go too far, then watch out. The hut we were billeted in was by the side of the River Isar which flowed through Bolzano at a rate of knots. There was an island in the river nearly opposite the camp and this is where most of us worked. The island was almost entirely composed of rounded stones which had been swept down over the years by the torrential river. Our job was to collect these stones and put them into a concrete mixer with a few bags of cement. This mixture was then tipped into a small truck running on lines of about two foot gauge and pushed over a narrow, spindly bridge and into the tunnel that some day would be the Roma Berlin Autostrada. The tunnel sloped downhill slightly, so for half a mile or so the two of you doing this job would stand on the back of the truck as it rumbled down through the darkness. About half a mile into the tunnel you could see the the circle of light where the Italian workers would be waiting for it. They used the contents of the truck to line the tunnel. The method was simple they had a collection of curved metal plates, or formers which could be bolted together in an arch following the shape of the tunnel. Starting at ground level the cement was shovelled behind the plate and once the cement came to the top of it another section would be bolted on and the process was repeated until they met at the top of the arch. Theoretically our job was designed so that a supply of cement would arrive in a steady stream but we saw to it that this never happened. It was generally all or nothing. This was easy to arrange as we could derail a truck whenever we wanted and could spend so much time getting it back on the rails that other trucks would be piled up behind us.

It became a very leisurely job especially as the Italians were not workaholics themselves. They only needed two sentries to keep an eye on everyone, one on the landward side of the bridge where he could look down on the island and the torrential Isar, and one at the tunnel entrance. There was also a sentry in the tunnel where the work was going on, but this one was unnecessary as there was only one entrance to the tunnel. And although we didn't mind him going to sleep, we objected to him leaving his rifle leaning against the scaffolding where we unloaded. We regretted our action later, because the Italian sentries on the whole were quite decent towards us, but at the time we thought it was adding insult to injury and took umbrage, and we started putting a little bit of cement down the barrel every time we had the opportunity. In fact production rates went up until we completed this task. We never saw that particular sentry again and as nothing was said to us we had to ask one of the other sentries where he had gone. We were told he had been issued with stockings, which was their way of saying that he had been posted to the Russian Front.

From the hut we lived in we had a grandstand view of lots of air raids, in fact it was too much like a ringside seat for comfort. Bolzano was on the route for a lot of the supplies coming to Italy by rail over the Brenner Pass and the bridge over the River Isar was constantly being bombed and repaired and bombed and repaired. For a time we had an 88mm anti aircraft gun sited on the island about a hundred yards away from the concrete mixer. One time during a daylight raid when we were on the island we made a mock up gun of our own. It was a pretty basic affair simply a pair of battered wheels and an axle which had been swept down river. With one wheel on the ground and a length of piping wedged in the top wheel as the upward pointing barrel it could be traversed most realistically. Large stones were passed along as ammunition and on the command "Fire!" the side of the concrete mixer was given a whang with a length of timber. Unfortunately our efforts to help were not appreciated and after the raid was over our gun was consigned to the Isar.

It was our misfortune to be in this camp in September 43 when Italy capitulated. Unlike many other camps further South where the prisoners were released and often helped on their way by the locals, here we knew nothing until bullets started coming through the hut. Fortunately because of a bank of earth they started at about six foot up and although some of the occupants of the top bunks had near escapes all survived. And as the Italians went out of the camp at one end German troops arrived at the other. It was heart breaking.

The day after we were in Germany.

CHAPTER 8

The Germany we were shipped to, in Upper Silesia, was a nation existing on the forced labour of millions. Every country that Hitler had over run provided their quota of slaves. They were half starved, poorly clad, ill shod, cowed and expendable. Some such as the Russians and any intelligentsia were more expendable than others. It was estimated that over four million Russians died. Compared with them we - approximately 140,000 British and Commonwealth PoWs- were living in luxury. Because Britain had German prisoners, the Geneva Conventions were more or less adhered to in relation to the British. We were well clothed as we had issues of battle dress and boots sent out to us. Not only did we look like soldiers but we thought and acted like them, and had our own NCOs in charge so that military standards were maintained and the camps were well run and organised on military lines. We fed better because of the Red Cross food parcels which we received even if sporadically and, above all, because we were confident of winning the war our morale was high, and it showed.

In 1943 the Germans hoped, because of the secret weapon that was always being promised, they might win the war but we knew we would. In the Stalag we were sent to we met men who had been captured at Dunkirk and in the Norwegian campaign and they told us how the mood of the Germans had changed from the arrogance of the early days when the swastika flew over most of Europe, with Hitler's 'Thousand - Years Reich' apparently a formality, to the subdued mood of foreboding of the present day.

Our attitude was shown in our actions. One of these was typical and I have no doubt similar actions happened in every Stalag with British PoWs. The Germans often had snap searches when everyone was turned out into the small exercise area while they went through the huts we lived in looking for signs of escape attempts or radios. It was just accepted as part of our way of life until someone got the idea-- if they want to search why not give them something to find? So word had gone out that there was a need for wire, any bits of wire. The end result was that any wire that came to hand from working parties that went out all disappeared via the hut leaders. When the Germans had their next snap search we were turfed out into the exercise area and they disappeared, as normal, into our huts. Then great excitement emanated from one of them - they had found a radio. At least they thought so - they had found a bit of wire showing in the ceiling of the hut, and they were away. The wire they had found was twisted to another length of wire and that to another and so they went on, down the ceiling of that hut and under the floor of the next one, then down the ceiling of the next one. By now they knew it wouldn't be a radio at the end of it, but with their thorough Teutonic nature they continued. The wire finally ended in the exercise area where we were waiting. There, surrounded by an appreciative audience, they dug down a few inches to find a Red Cross parcel box. The sole contents was a slip of paper with a catch phrase of the day written on it, a "You've had it, chums."

For that, we had the maximum amount of roll calls that were allowed by the Geneva Conventions in a day, generally in the small hours of the morning. But as we weren't going anywhere no one minded. Though I have since thought if we had known what the Germans were capable of (for Auschwitz, where at least two million went the gas chambers, was only a few miles away) we might not have been so cocky.

Another incident of a similar kind happened when the Red Cross parcels stopped coming through. These breaks in supplies of Red Cross parcels and mail were generally caused by the disruption of rail traffic by bombing raids so there was a certain perverse satisfaction in these breaks but, although the mail was missed, the parcels were literally our life line. Food was normally our main topic of conversation but even more so when the supply of parcels stopped, and it was thoughts on these lines that triggered this incident off.

The huts we occupied were in rows but each in a separate compound. Every evening two sentries would enter the compound and after first locking the door of the hut they would go around the outside of the hut closing and barring the shutters. They were helped in this job by two ferocious Alsation dogs who came into the compound with them and bounded on ahead of them going for any prisoner who dawdled outside the hut. They obviously loved their work. This was an accepted procedure until some one posed the question, 'What if instead of the dogs biting us we bite the dogs?' Once the idea was raised, the plan to carry it out was inevitably put into action. Four volunteers – there were dozens – were padded by putting on extra borrowed battle dress over their own and a bunk was dismantled to provide each of them with three by three corner posts as blunt instruments. They waited at the bottom end of the hut out of sight of the guards. The Alsations, running ahead, went for the proffered, padded arms and once so occupied their end was short and sharp. Their skulls were battered in, the bodies thrown inside the hut where they were skinned, cut up and divided out almost before the guards had finished closing the shutters. Their whistles and calls for the dogs fell on deaf ears. It was only when the skins were thrown on the barbed wire fence the following day that the guards realised where they had disappeared to - well beyond the sound of a whistle.

The Stalag we were in, though mainly occupied by British, had men from all the Commonwealth countries who had fought in almost every theatre of war: France, Norway, Greece, Crete, Africa, Eritrea and Italy. And there were even a few naval ratings and Merchant Navy men. The stories they had to tell were many and varied. "When I get out I'll write a book," was a common phrase and lots of them certainly had the material. I met an American who had been in the crew of one of the Flying Fortress's that we had watched as they bombed the bridge at Bolzano. I remember a Guardsman who was nicknamed Bridgehead because he talked so often of the landing at the Anzio Bridgehead.

But of all the hundreds of stories I must have heard, and we talked shop a lot, I can only remember three. One was told me by an Australian and I am sure I remembered it because I myself do not like confined spaces and it seemed, at a time when thousands died terrible deaths, one of the worst ways to go. The Australian had been captured in Greece and a few hundred of them had been crammed into a walled court yard. One of them had found a manhole cover which he pulled up and dropped down a few feet into the hole he had uncovered. The bottom was a junction with a large drain. Saying he could see light at the end of it he started squirming his way down towards the end of it. He was soon followed by others and although they placed a blanket over the top of the hole and started a game of cards there were so many congregated about it that the commotion attracted the Germans' attention. Their reaction was immediate and brutal. They dropped a grenade down the hole and then, going to the outer end of the drain, now choc a bloc with men, they fired a machine gun into it. All of which they were entitled to under the Geneva Conventions because they were prisoners of war attempting escape. The Aussie who told the story reckoned the drain was so long that some must have been untouched, and consequently literally buried alive.

The other incident was told me by a New Zealander who had been captured at Crete. They had been having breakfast in an olive grove as the first German parachutists started dropping down amongst them and they started picking them off as they dangled in their parachutes. Later the troop carrying gliders started landing. One of them landed close to them but no one got out and after a time when things got a little quieter they went across to have look at it. The German troops were still strapped in it but as the glider had landed it had hit a shelf of rock and they were all sheared off at the ankles.

The other story Bomber told me and I remember it because it summed up exactly the classic description of war - long periods of boredom with short periods of violent activity. The gun team he served with in the 31st Field Regiment in Eritrea was moving along the bottom of a valley in the heat of the day. As the squad and the gun rumbled along the dusty track all except the driver were dozing and somnolent in the heat, some asleep in the comfort of the camouflage netting. All this ended suddenly when an Italian gun team came into sight over a slight rise about two hundred yards from them, almost a mirror image of themselves at point blank range. They got the order "Action front" at the same time as the equivalent order must have been given in Italian. From sleep and somnolence to ferocious action. It takes about two minutes to unlimber a gun and get it into action and it must have seemed a very long two minutes. But all the years of training and seemingly endless gun drills in India came into their own. Theirs was the first shot fired and that was the only one that mattered. They buried the Italians and were content to be alive to tell the tale.

It was from this Stalag that I saw a example of how King's Rules and Regulations worked. There was a good leavening of regular soldiers amongst us and on this particular day there was one with us, Anderson, a 'hard man' though not very bright - still a gunner though nearly due for a pension. He had almost done his twenty one years, or pontoon, which is what they joined up for in those days - a 'pontoon' after the score in the card game of that name. There were about twenty of us who had been sent out on some fatigue and we were ambling along the road as slowly as possible with the two sentries trying to get us to move a little faster. Quite suddenly in a voice that brooked no objection the order was barked out from Anderson "March to attention!" . We reacted instinctively and, looking down the road, we saw the reason. A hundred yards away from us, also with a couple of sentries, was the crew of a shot down bomber shambling dispiritly towards us. Shamble was the word for the clumsy boots and bulky jackets they were wearing were designed to keep a body warm at high levels and were not designed for marching in. It was amongst this crew Anderson had seen the peaked hat of an officer. King's rules and regulations laid down that all officers must be saluted. And to this he reacted automatically. If there were no NCOs to take charge of the section this duty fell to that of the oldest soldier. That was him, he was the oldest soldier. He had us swinging down the road with our boots crashing down in unison as if we were on a British barrack square with the surprised sentries left behind. Anderson's voice kept us up to it. Left. Left. Left. Then in a voice for our ears only, "Now watch this, eyes right or I'll have your guts for garters. Left. Left. Eeeeyes Right! " Twenty heads went around as one. Anderson's salute snapped up. The flying officer may not have had much saluting drill but he had enough and his hand went up in acknowledgment. We went past him as if he was on a saluting base. "Eeeeeyes left!" Our heads swung back. "March easy," and we reverted to our ambling and the startled sentries caught us up. Behind us the aircrew shambled on but I 'm sure they got the message. They might be down but they weren't out.

A short time after this incident we were sent out on our first regular working party. It was to a sugar beet factory. In a way it was a microcosm of how the Third Reich kept going. The factory itself was surrounded by a high wall topped with barbed wire and there were sentries to see we stayed on the inside of it. The sentries were all troops who were no longer fit for active service and on the whole our relationship with them was quite good. On occasions, when the the reason for them being there was not apparent, we would ask them why they were there and not on the Russian front, and they would invariably press the tops of their boot down to its sole with their rifle butt. One got the feeling they considered themselves the lucky ones. They had been to the Russian front, Hitler's fridge, and except for being minus their toes they had got back in one piece and wanted to stay that way.

All the gangers were men too old for the army and most of them had total power over their workers none of whom had anyone to back them up. For them the Geneva Conventions did not apply. There were gangs of teenage Polish girls some of whom I realised must have been about the same age as my sister at home. They dressed in the same drab makeshift clothes as the other prisoners did but occasionally you would see one who had managed to get a piece of brighter coloured material for use as a head band or a scarf. It may have been a statement of femininity but it was also a brave gesture, letting the world know she hadn't been beaten.

It was the Russian prisoners of war who provided most of the labour. It was estimated that there were five million of them and they could be worked to death. And about four million were. There were also work parties of Czechoslovakian Jews who had a yellow star sewn onto their rags. We always tried to contact them for a few words. Many were English speakers and almost all had been in the professions or arts. Now we know it was the Germans method of getting rid of the Czech elite. The prisoners' problem was to stay fit enough to work as the alternative was the gas chambers. The Germans had to have gangs, as no one could be trusted to work on their own. The few prisoners who did work on their own were generally French who had been among the first to arrive and whose families were in German occupied France. On the whole they seemed to be the best off of all the foreign prisoners as they worked mainly on farms where food could be acquired and they did not have guards. Some Poles also worked alone but with hindsight one cannot blame the latter.

Fifteen per cent of the population of Poland died at the hands of the Germans and concessions as regards extra food must have been a tremendous temptation.

The gangers we had were a mixed bag, from fanatical Nazis, the Herrensvolk, the Master Race who believed the propaganda that was still being pushed out about the ultimate secret weapon that would win the war for them and was just around the corner, to those who realised that they were losing the war but dare not say what they thought. All at one time or another would shake a newspaper before us when there was a headline telling of some German victory but we soon found the answer. We would take the paper off them and turn it over. In the rows of classified columns on the back page there was always a sizable section written in heavy Gothic script and interspersed with heavy black crosses, each marking the name of some local man who had died for Fuehrer and Fatherland. As we had all picked up a bit of German we could easily get across that the front page was propaganda but the last page was facts . It never failed. They had no answer to that.

In the propaganda stakes the Red Cross parcels were an indisputable trump card. There were two types of Red Cross food parcels, British and Canadian. Both of them 10lb in weight and both had a standard set of contents and there was an on going discussion as to which was the best. The Canadian one with its North American style packaging certainly looked the best but packaging meant weight and could not be eaten. However both were more than welcome, they were lifesavers. If it had not been for them we would have died at the same rate as the Russians.

One of the main differences between the British and Canadian type of parcel was that the British one had a packet of tea in it and the Canadian one a packet of coffee. Bean coffee as the Germans called it, something they hadn't seen for years. As few English drank coffee in those days it was ideal for trading with. We didn't care for it and they craved for it and, as it was a rural area, most of them kept hens and would willingly give about three dozen eggs for a packet of coffee, plus running a not inconsiderable risk. Soap was the only non-edible item in the parcels and that, a luxury item in Germany, also found a ready market. The propaganda side was a bonus. Even the colourful good quality packaging was saying it had come from another world.

The main interest we had besides food was sabotage. It wasn't desperate stuff, just a steady nibbling away. Anything that could be broken or damaged was. Losing or breaking tools. Emptying the fire buckets of sand into the vats of sugar and filling the buckets with brown sugar with a sprinkling of sand on top. There was a dump of coal briquettes which we got in the habit of throwing over the perimeter wall. We did this a few times, then realised we couldn't hear them hitting the ground. The answer was obvious - there were people on the other side catching them as we threw them over. This became very popular when we had willing German accomplices getting rid of the evidence.

Though most of the sugar beet arrived in railway trucks, some came by carts from local farms drawn by oxen and horses. There always seemed to be someone who knew a little more than normal about most things and it was in this case. Someone knew that raw sugar beet is no good for horses, even if the horses do not know it. So with this knowledge we saw to it that they had plenty of opportunity to indulge themselves. We realised that this sort of sabotage must be happening all over Germany when a railway truck arrived that was filled with the remains of a wrecked plane, with only a covering of sugar beet on top. It must have taken whoever was responsible hours of work and we were filled with admiration for them. On our part a lot of energy was expended to see that their efforts were not wasted and that the entire contents of that truck went into the channels of water that swept the sugar beet into the factory for processing. As the first process was a series of knives which chopped up the beet we managed to stop production for a time until the damaged cutters were either replaced or resharpened.

We also instigated a strike here but we had little success. Because we were striking for more food everyone in the factory backed it, even if they had some trepidation as to the outcome. They were not disappointed. The plan was that everyone sat tight in the mess hall and we asked for more food. The strike was broken quickly, simply and brutally. The guards came in and as each nationality had a tendency to stick together they took one nationality at a time and went in with rifle butts and boots, starting with the Russians. The British were the last to get this treatment and it was noticeable that we, the instigators, received the most lenient treatment.

The work at the sugar beet factory was seasonal so there came a time when everything was dismantled, cleaned and reassembled ready for the next season. Our final job before we returned to the Stalag was to clean the pipes that ran throughout the factory. We did this, had them checked by the ganger and then reassembled them after first stuffing all the cleaning rags, or anything else we could find that was suitable, into them.

Back at the Stalag we had an amazing offer. It was on a poster which appeared on the notice board overnight and was asking for volunteers to join the Free British Corp. This Free British Corp the poster told us, would fight on the Eastern Front side by side with their German comrades in arms against the common enemy of the West, Bolshevism. The reaction couldn't have been what the Germans expected. For days people were going around clicking their heels together, giving the Nazi salute and Heil Hitlering to all and sundry, to Feldwebel Armstrong, Gruppen Fuehrer Johnson or Herr General Tompkins.

We didn't have long to consider this offer before about sixty of us were moved again. This time it was to a small work camp attached to an open cast coal mine. About a third of the prisoners with us were South Africans. The English speaking South Africans were entirely volunteers, whereas many of the Afrikaaners had been policemen and were members of the SA Police Brigade who could only be called upon to serve anywhere in Africa. A South African sergeant major was sent with us as camp leader, also a medical orderly, neither of whom went out to work. Both of them were Afrikaans speakers which was equivalent of saying they could speak German, which was for the common good as they could argue our case much better.

About this time we had a reminder of the outside world and the war that was going on there, though it was only later we knew the significance. We woke one morning to find the whole country side littered with narrow strips of aluminium foil. It was obviously not German but we knew there must be some reason for it and it cheered us up and no doubt conversely depressed the Germans. Much later we found the strips had been dropped to confuse the German radar.

All the work took place in a huge open cast mine. Which ever way you looked you could see a dark brownish cliff. We worked in gangs of about fifteen with a sentry to see we didn't leave and a foreman to see we worked. The best foreman by far from our point of view was one we called Wallace Beery, after an American film star of the day because that is who he looked like. Most of us had picked up some German by now and during the food breaks we would have conversations with him and he once told us with explanatory actions and hearty guffaws that there was an Iron Cross for Damen, first class if they had eight children, second class for seven and third class if they only had six.

One of the other foremen had been called back from his retirement and the thought that the mine couldn't operate without him had gone to his head. He was a thin boney individual with sunken cheeks and had one of the popular Hitler style moustache's. To avoid the rough going, he always walked balancing along the railway lines. We never once saw him lose his balance. Because of his skeletal appearance we had nicknamed him Drei Fittel Tod, three quarter dead. This was abbreviated to Drei Fittel and when Wallace Beery, who had no love for him, found out he laughed so much we thought he would have an apoplexy. But the bane of our life was the mine manager, the Green Shadow. There had been a popular pre war film called the Red Shadow. He was a tall lean dynamo of a man, in his thirties and strong as a horse. He got his nickname because he wore a long loose green loden coat which was always streaming out cloaklike behind him as he covered the ground at a rate of knots. We never knew whether he was motivated to work so hard for the good of the Third Reich or for his own good, working so hard to make himself indispensable and so keep him away from the Eastern Front. If it was the latter it was to no avail as it wasn't long before the front came to him. He also had the misapprehension to think that others such as us should work as he did. We did our best to show him otherwise.

We had not been in this work camp very long when the South African medical orderly found that the Germans in their methodical way had made allowances for a certain percentage in the camp to be on the sick list. It was probably laid down in the Geneva Conventions, so a roster was drawn up to see that they were not disappointed . Initially this 'sick' list was well patronised, then, because of the worries of some about the repercussions of this if they were caught out malingering, this list was not always taken up. A small hard core, which included Bomber and myself, having no such qualms, spent a lot of time 'sick'. Cap Barron, a South African and a close friend of Bomber and myself, was another one. Cap was from a small village called Weenan which he told me was Afrikaans for weeping because the Boers of some ox wagon train had been massacred there. He said when war was declared both he and his elder brother who ran a farm between them because their parents were dead, could not agree as to who should run the farm and who should join up. They agreed to sleep on it and decide in the morning but during the night Cap, with the idea of 'fait accompli', got up and drove about a hundred odd miles to the nearest recruiting station where he met his brother who had had the same idea. Neither went back to the farm. Cap had had an odd upbringing, having been brought up by native servants and he spoke Zulu before English. He once told me that as a child he had been brought up with a rifle as his only plaything and there had been unlimited game to use it on.

Another man who was also on the sick list quite a lot seemed to us a very elderly (he was probably forty) South African called George Dykes. A volunteer, he had had to say he was younger than he was to get into the army. He was a very popular man with an easy going manner but differed from most in his attitude to Red Cross parcels. To everyone else they meant food, but to George they meant drink. The raisins, the prunes and the sugar were what George really wanted and he would trade other things in the parcel to get these items. Getting yeast was his problem. To get his brews fermenting, he was always experimenting and he did once try carbide, which we could get from the mine. But on the whole he managed through trading. Often the sentries must have wondered how George could get plastered inside the wire and they were hard put to do that outside it

During my time on the sick list the NCO in charge, a South African sergeant, taught me to play chess. I spent a lot of time trying to beat him. We were together when we saw an incident that incensed us. Behind the camp was a gloomy regimented pine forest and immediately behind the camp itself a square about the size of three football pitches had been cleared in it. It was used by the Hitler Youth organisation for gliding instruction, using a small powered winch to get the gliders up. This had been one of the methods Hitler had used to circumvent the restrictions of the Versailles Treaty imposed on Germany after the 1914-18 war. Not allowed to have an air force, he had set up Flying Clubs and gliding schools throughout the country which formed the basis of the Luftwaffe. A footpath ran across this field from corner to corner, obviously from some farm or hamlet in the forest, and we saw people using it from time to time on their way to the village. The women (we never saw any men) wore a traditional type of peasant dress and we had been told they were a small ethnic group called Venns. On this occasion two members of the Hitler Jugend, an obligitary military organisation for German youth between thirteen and eighteen, in uniform as always, and probably fourteen or fifteen years old, were occupying themselves by the shed that housed the glider and winch. An elderly woman came out of the forest and started trudging her way slowly across the field. She had almost reached the road that led to the village when they stopped her. From the distance we could see her point to the road barely twenty yards away. It was to no avail. They pointed back the way she had come, they were the Master Race. She never argued, just turned mutely around and started making her way slowly back. She appeared much later, having walked around the two sides of the field. There was a lot of that attitude about in the Hitler Youth organisation. I remembered it later when I had a rifle in my hands.

Fortunately Bomber and I had had the forethought to have a long session with the medical orderly as to what we should say if any German medical staff arrived at the camp and when a German medical officer did turn up unexpectedly on a day I had reported sick I knew the symptoms of sinuses by heart. I was sent off to hospital and my luck held by an amazing coincidence. The majority of medical orderlies at the hospital were British and one of them, Jim Barlow, was from my home town, Radcliffe, where pre-war he had been a promising light weight boxer. We had time for a chat about the old home town and I realised how lucky I was when he told me how many Russians they had to treat with self-inflicted injuries. They did it to get away from the misery of their camps and for the chance of a bit more food. He told me they generally started with the little finger of the left hand and went on from there. Some had sacrificed three fingers. The method they used was to put the finger on a railway line and let a railway truck run over it.

Jim saw to it that I saw the right people and I left with confirmation that I was genuine and suffering from sinuses. I returned to the camp to find I had missed out on an odd hangover from peace time Germany. They had been visited by an elderly photographer from the nearby town of Hoyerswerda and some group photographs had been taken. He had been paid in the useless paper money we were paid with and with which we could buy nothing except, as it turned out, a photograph. It was as if he was a leftover from another age that had been overlooked in the scheme of things. Total war had passed him by.

The work we were doing most of the time was moving and relaying railway lines in a huge open cast coal mine, perhaps the one that had supplied the briquettes we had thrown away so generously. It was winter time with snow on the ground and as it was often snowing a crow bar or a spanner had only to be laid down for a moment for the snow to cover it and it disappeared, so the job was constantly being held up as we waited or looked for tools. A plus point at this time was that we were receiving Red Cross parcels regularly. Instead of using the much bombed and consequently unreliable German railway system the International Red Cross were delivering the parcels in convoys of white trucks with red crosses painted on them. The Swiss drivers delivered the parcels direct to the Stalags from where they were distributed a relatively short distance to the work camps. Soap and coffee came into their own again. The extra food was more than welcome and there is no doubt it kept a lot of us alive as the winter of 1945 was exceptional and the weather was bitter to the extreme. Twenty below was common. Every morning when we woke up there would be fingers of frost four or five inches long on the ends of the metal bolts that held the hut together.

Signs of the war were more obvious. Sometimes we would be working near the main railway line and could see supplies en route to the Eastern front, the most obvious being white painted tanks and guns. I suppose Bomber and I weren't the only ones who thought about trying to get on board one and playing it by ear when we got to the front but as far as I know only two managed to even get started. They were a couple of regular gunners nicknamed Pinky and Mush who were in another work camp in the area. They managed to get into a railway truck on one of the trains and had hidden themselves under the tarpaulin but unfortunately once on board and the train moving they relaxed, confident they could not be seen, and they forgot about the men in the signal cabins. They had barely gone a few miles before they were recaptured.

Another sign of the times was the sight of the terrified refugees from the East fleeing before the advancing Red Army. The Nazi propaganda of previous years when they excused

POWs at Arbeits Kommanden (works camp) 77146. Bomber is standing second from the left. The wood behind is the type we escaped into.

themselves for the slaughter of Russians because they were bestial subhumans who thought only of rape and pillage had backfired. Now these bestial subhumans were in Germany and the German and German colonists who had been settled on land in the East remembered past propaganda and were fleeing before them. They passed through the area in an endless column, often their carts were drawn by cows and many were harnessed three abreast as troikas. Some had hoops above their head collars which I suppose in happier times had carried bells or ribbons. In the ups and downs of life, one man's misfortune being another man's good fortune, we had an absolute windfall when one of their horses died just as it was passing by the camp. I suppose the owner was fortunate in the fact that it must have been one of the few places in Europe where he could have sold a dead horse for anything worthwhile. The South African camp leader with his command of German successfully pleaded our case with the Camp Commandant and managed to get permission to trade for the carcass with English cigarettes. After the deal was successfully concluded we ate like lords for a time.

It was shortly after this windfall that Bomber and I were given the doubtful honour of being picked out as the slowest workers in the gang. We were pretty sure it was bestowed on us by the Green Shadow and we knew why. We had been with a gang of about eight 'unloading' a truck of sand, six of them shovelling it out and Bomber and I had got the idea of shovelling it back, when the Green Shadow appeared on the scene as if from nowhere.

The end result was that we were sent to what was called a straaf laager or punishment camp. We had a companion on this trip, a small pleasant South African solicitor called Roger, who had obviously never had to do any manual work in his life, and no matter how hard he tried, he was ineffectual. His ganger had taken a dislike to him and his fate was sealed. The punishment camp was in a quarry and we were the only English speakers there. I think every European language was spoken, with German as the common language.

There was a much higher proportion of guards here and all

of them had been incapacitated in some way or the other, most as usual had lost toes through frostbite and walked with difficulty. The routine in the quarry was simple. Every morning the quarry men blasted and the task of each prisoner was to break up enough of the fallen rock with a sledge hammer to fill six tipper trucks that carried about a square metre of broken rock each. When that was done he was finished for the day and could return to the barrack hut. Our companions, weak as they were, went at this task as fast as their strength would allow and one by one disappeared back to the barracks. By midday Bomber and 1, who could see no attraction in returning to the camp, were still gently tapping away, along with Roger, doing his ineffectual best, and would be the only ones left, with about eight sentries watching over us. The sentries themselves never tried to make us work harder and one got the feeling that their orders were simply to see we did not escape. All they wanted to do was keep out of mischief until the war was over and they could go home. This became the regular pattern and sometimes as they got cold or bored the sentries themselves would take a sledge hammer and break a few rocks themselves. So in this leisurely manner we filled our quota.

It was because of this method that we saw Dresden being bombed. It was midday and we three and about eight sentries were all that were left in the quarry when we became conscious of the powerful drone of distant engines approaching. Soon we could see the vapour trails of hundreds of B 17s, Flying Fortresses, overhead. It was an awe inspiring sight with the sound of the engines now overwhelming and ominous to the ninth degree. We could hear the whine of the lighter engines of German and American fighters and I now know that the Germans were totally out fought and out numbered five to one by the seven hundred long range Mustangs that were riding shot gun over the 1500 Fortresses and which had made these raids into the heart of Germany possible. We could hear distant machine gun fire but all seemed incidental. The overall feeling was of an irresistible force, too powerful to be distracted from its mission by pinpricks. Even the hundreds of undeviating vapour trails left by the planes had an arrogance about them as if saying, here we are. What are you going to do about it?

From the entrance to the quarry we could look down on to Dresden and I remember vividly when they unloaded their bombs that even the distant sound was such that I thought no one, but no one, should be underneath that. Yet another side of me was exulting and saying, 'Serve the bastards right.'

The sound of the engines faded, rumbling away in the distance like a passing storm. A few descending parachutes carrying their occupants to an uncertain fate, the fading vapour trails and the cloud over what had been Dresden told of their passing. We returned to the barracks in silence We were all, prisoners and guards, stunned by what we had seen. When our sentence at the strafe laager was finished we went back the way we had come, through Dresden. When we had arrived we had passed through the streets of a pleasant almost mediaeval town busy with people and traffic, even if mainly horse drawn. We returned through a heap of rubble. The rubble came down to the middle of the street and here there was a narrow footpath, space for a cyclist or a wheelbarrow or one person, and everyone you saw still had the trace of shock on their face. One hundred and thirty-five thousand people, twenty-five per cent of the population, died in Dresden, more than at Hiroshima. There were not enough left to bury their own dead. In later years people say it shouldn't have happened, but that's with hindsight. At the time, and having by now seen what the Nazis had done and what Nazism meant, I was all for it. Send it down, David, was my sentiment.

My last letter from a prison camp was sent about three weeks later.

'*Dear Faraway Folks.*

This is penned and posted in the forlorn hope that it will make the grade but Ah hae ma doots, going on the assumption that if mail cannot come to us it will not be able to leave us. Mail is referred to by us in the past tense, three months past. There is no doubt about it it is a queer show and in a way I am lucky to have a ringside seat, though I suppose that is a debatable point. The way things are it reminds me of a dog chasing its tail, you can see the end but it never gets any closer. But some day it will all be over and I will spin you some yarns and you will tell me "not to pull your leg". You will fry bacon and eggs, three years past tense and apple dumplings, tie my tie (I have forgotten) a drink with Dad, go to a dance and have a holiday all on my own. I have never been on my own for four years and you would never believe how much I long for a bit of solitude 'far from the haunts of men ' and all that kind of stuff. My best wishes I trust you take for granted and if this is a lucky letter and does reach home convey my greetings to all I know and above all don't worry, that is the main thing, nothing really matters and one of these days you will be having an old fashioned Rip van Winkle on charge again. So I will fold up my love and luck and send it to you whilst waiting for 'der Tag', yours Mick.'

CHAPTER 9

Bomber, Cap and myself had always had the idea that when conditions looked right we would make a run for it. The opportunity when it came was amazingly quick, in fact we almost missed our chance.

The three of us were members of a work party marching out to some job or other. Unusually the roads were crowded, for there were hordes of refugees with their carts and livestock streaming the other way when a Russian plane appeared and came down the road strafing. It was instant chaos for everyone, sentries included, dived for cover. When we got to our feet we realised the opportunity we had missed, for there was a dense pine wood not more than two hundred yards away. As we were berating ourselves for lack of initiative we got a second chance as another plane followed the first.

We didn't hesitate this time. We just took off. Another prisoner, a South African called 'Rosie' Johnson took the same chance and the four of us literally ran for our lives. We were almost into the cover of the wood when bullets started coming our way. Rosie was the unlucky one and he fell wounded or dead. We never saw him again. (Rosie had got his nickname from playing the part of a girl, Rosie, in some army show in a South Africa). I hope he made it back.

We kept on going, confident that we wouldn't be bothered for some time as the sentries could not leave the rest of the party. The wood was one of the huge pine woods that covered so much of Upper Silesa, easy to keep going in, yet with ample cover if we got down low. We slowed down soon and late in the afternoon we came upon a narrow dirt road and a deserted cart. Judging from its contents it had been abandoned by some refugees. Why it had been left we had no idea. To us it meant one thing, a chance of some food. But the cart hadn't a lot to offer. All that had been left foodwise by its owners was a box of a dozen eggs which had been overlooked under some bedding and a large bottle of vinegar. It was here I received a physics lesson for when we started to boil the eggs in the vinegar the ascetic acid softened the shells. To one who had never done physics at school, interesting.

And so we lived. We were always heading east through what seemed a deserted world and always looking for food, though Cap was now desperate for a cigarette. We had a fortunate escape once when we laid in a clearing by the side of a river and dozed off in the sun. Bomber suddenly woke us up and with a, "Quick, come on!" he disappeared into the trees. We didn't hesitate. We just followed and in the wood he told us that just as he woke up a German soldier had appeared in the field on the opposite bank of the river. He had a towel around his neck and was obviously intending to have a wash in the river but he also had his rifle slung over his shoulder. He had stopped opposite the small clearing where we were, seen us and unslung his rifle. Our battle dress was not greatly different in colour from the brown smocks of the Russians and his reasoning had obviously been, three Russians . . . only forty yards. I can get one, probably two, but the third is doubtful. I am in a field totally devoid of cover so he may get me. I'll go and get help. Bomber with his cap over his eyes had just laid there motionless feigning sleep and watched him as he trotted off up the slope and over the crest of the hill. A few minutes later from the cover of the wood we watched the German return with half a dozen others. The fact that he was carrying his rifle when he went for a wash made us certain that we were getting close to the

Russian lines.

Later we had another incident that told us even more emphatically that we were getting close to the Russians. In fact we were in no mans land. We had gone into a house on a cross roads and as usual had gone in to it to see what it had to offer. We had no luck either as regards food or cigarettes, when we heard the sound of a motor bike approaching. Just to be on the safe side, for we could not tell whether it was friend or foe, we went through the house and into a shed behind it where we all sat down. The sound of the engine came closer, then stopped outside the house. Soon after we could hear voices and we knew they whoever they were - were in the house doing exactly what we had been doing a few minutes previously - seeing what it had to offer, But we couldn't make out what language they were speaking. We also realised we were in a tricky situation. If we had been asked to choose the most stupid things to sit on we couldn't have improved on what we had chosen. Bomber was sitting on a upturned bucket which besides cutting a perfect circle in his-behind, clinked at his slightest movement; Cap had sat on an unsteady pile of firewood and I was on a sack of coke that creaked at my every breath.

Help came from an unexpected quarter. Another motor bike could be heard approaching the scene. We heard our fellow occupants dash outside and drag their bike inside. Their conversation stopped and all was silent. The sound of the approaching bike came closer, then it also stopped outside, and we heard the sound of voices as its two riders entered the house. There was a short burst of machine gun fire, more indistinct voices, and shortly afterwards the sound of two motor bike engines fading away. We went back into the house and found the bodies of two dead Germans.

Obviously we were getting warm. Cap went through their pockets to see if they had any cigarettes but had no luck The Russians had obviously beaten him to it. We moved on, Bomber still rubbing his behind, in the same direction as the motor bike.

It was about now that Cap left us. Desperate for a smoke, he went to go and see if he could find cigarettes in a small hamlet that we could see in the distance and he never came back. I know he survived the war because I was told he turned up at the village of a particular friend of his in the North of England. He had handed the landlord of the local two hundred pounds (a lot of money in those days) with the instructions to let him know when it was used up. When that day came, he shook hands with his friend and said farewell to the many he had drunk with and left for South Africa.

So then Bomber and I were alone in our search for the Russians. We never found them but all ended well because they found us. We had had discussions as to the best method to make contact - keep under cover until we saw them or walk down the middle of the road so they could see us. We were using the latter system when we made contact. They came from behind us on bikes and we never heard anything until one gave a sort of grunt. We turned round and saw two of them standing astride their bikes with their carbines pointing at us. I was more than glad that we had had the forethought to get a Russian prisoner to coach us parrot fashion in the phrase, "I am an escaped English prisoner." Parrot fashion perhaps but word perfect. In reply to our party piece one of the Russians grinned and pointed down the road we had just come down. They were point men.

Shades of the Italians in Africa. And so we joined the Russian army. It was standard procedure for odds and sods like us to be passed back behind the lines, but when we let them know we would like to stay they had no objections. I remember the final word was given by a type of political officer. Thinking back he probably thought of us as two western capitalist lackeys who could get killed. They gave us rifle each and we drifted with the rest.

That is what we seemed to do, drift, just moving forward until some one fired at us. One evening when we were with them we were close to a village that was on fire, and some horse-drawn transport passed between us and the burning village so that they were silhouetted against the flames. We were sitting there eating. On its own it was an exceptional chiaroscuro but what lifted it into something far more memorable was that some one on one of the carts was playing a sad evocative Russian tune on an accordion. It gave the incident another dimension which helped fix it in my memory.

We must have gone through dozens of villages all with their own little incidents but in only two can I remember anything specific. In one we found we were sharing it with a large German patrol whom Bomber, a Russian and myself watched them go down the opposite side of the street from a bedroom window. It was an odd feeling to see Germans so close but in the circumstances, more of them than us, we considered discretion the better part of valour. It was very shortly after this incident that we entered a small village and had come to the conclusion that it was unoccupied. After we had satisfied ourselves on that score we were doing our own thing, collecting items for what we called our swag bag. I suppose loot is the correct term. As always on the lookout for food, we were searching around in the last house in the village, a farm, and as I looked across the farmyard into a barn I saw through a gap in the barn doors a German. He was cycling slowly along the road towards the village with his rifle slung. I drew Bomber's attention to him and his one comment was, "If he goes any slower he'll fall over." We passed the information on to a Russian who was with us and all three of us were standing in the farmyard by the wall of the barn when the German came into view. The Russian gave a little grunt and the German looked towards us. To me he looked old, probably mid-forties. I noticed he had medal ribbons, one of which was bright yellow and I thought that yellow must have different connotations for them. Then the Russian squeezed the trigger and he came to the end of the line.

Why we stayed there I have no idea for that German - he was point man - had done just what he was supposed to do, contact the enemy. It was certain he wouldn't be on his own. We were still there looking for eggs when the tracers that were coming into the barn set the hay in it on fire. After that we were away and were going down the village clearing garden fences like steeple chasers when Bomber reminded me we had forgotten the swag bag. I told him he could have my share if he went back and he replied he'd think about it. It was sometime about now our brains started working and we got rid of our Russian carbines and ammunition. It was in the nick of time. As we dropped over the last garden wall we found about six of our erstwhile comrades surrounded by about twenty Germans. The young officer in charge, whose insignia told us he had once been an anti aircraft gunner, spoke near fluent English, with a far better accent than my North country one. He had studied at Cambridge and when we told him that we were P.o.Ws who had been picked up by the Russian patrol he accepted it without question. He said England and Germany should be fighting together to fight the common enemy, the barbarous Bolsheviks. We were to hear this again later but at the time I must confess we agreed wholeheartedly. We never saw our erstwhile Russian comrades again.

We ended up in solitary confinement, but with a difference. Instead of a cell to be alone in we had an entire prison. It had been a prison for the Luftwaffe but its last inmates had been cleared out and were now fighting in the Third Reich's last struggle. It was an eerie and unnerving experience. We were locked in adjoining cells and except for shell fire and bombing we could hear nothing, except, twice a day, distant doors would clang hollowly, opening and shutting and gradually getting closer as an old German brought our food. We had picked up enough German to get over to our gaoler that he must look after himself and not get himself killed. I am sure he appreciated the sincerity of our concern for his health. He was probably the only person who knew we were there and if anything happened to him we would have starved to death. I had a stump of a pencil in my pocket and the only pastime I had was to shoot down the squadrons of German planes M.E.s. Stukas, Focke Wulfs, Heinkels that had been drawn on the walls of my cell by previous inmates. They were all technically accurate but all were steadily going down in flames as I drew a Spitfire on their tails. To help pass the time I tried to ration myself to about one every hour.

We were taken from here, as the previous inmates had been, to help the Third Reich. Theoretically the job was simple enough, all we had to do was to get the rations to the troops. The cook house was in a railway tunnel and we had to pull a large dog cart loaded with milk churns full of soup to their front line. As the town was under fire it was not the best of jobs and we had a sentry to see we went there. On one trip when we were at the crest of a slight incline we thought an incoming shell was going to land too close for comfort so the three of us dived into the gutter for shelter. It was after the shell had exploded and we found we were all still in one piece that we lifted our heads up in time to see the loaded dog cart still gathering speed as it bumped its way down the slope, tip over at the bottom and deposit the cook's efforts into the gutter.

The Germans were billeted in a school, most of them in the relative security of the cellar, but we had the best room in the building, at least in peace time, the headmaster's study. This was a room with a view as it was on a corner of the first floor with windows on two sides and we thought, correctly, pretty vulnerable. It had two large photographs on the wall, one of Hindenburg the other of Hitler. We turned this one to the wall and the sentry just grinned. There came a time when we returned to this room and when Bomber opened the door there was no room there. It had been shot clean away. In the corridor everything as normal - open the door, and nothing. We looked straight down to the play ground. Never at a loss, Bomber flung the door wide and, with an elaborate 'after you', waved me in. The sentry thought this was a great joke.

Later we were standing in this playground, looking down on the road, about four or five feet below us, when a section of the Hitler Junger came marching by . There were about twelve of them all in uniform and in their mid teens with an arrogant young Youth Leader in charge. We heard a shell coming over and from experience calculated it wasn't going to bother us and stayed put. They also heard it and came to a different conclusion and dived for cover. The young leader was the first to get back on his feet and as he did so he looked up to see us sitting on our dog cart looking down at them. I have seldom seen anyone so incensed. He went berserk, screaming at his unfortunate section, kicking them to their feet, beside himself with rage. If you had been conditioned from childhood to believe you were the master race, things like that must have come very hard. On the other hand, if you are going to fight a war this is the way they should be indoctrinated, not sent to the Mickey Mouse club at the local cinema every Saturday morning. There were a lot of these brainwashed young fanatics about. Later we never gave them a second chance.

We had a conversation with the ex Cambridge man again later, along with four or five other young officers. They were just older versions of the Hitler Youth and obviously curious as to what the British looked like. All reiterated the idea that we should be fighting together against the common enemy Bolshevism. All had pinned their hopes on the secret weapon that Hitler had promised would bring them victory if they could just hang on, though I am sure they knew as well as we did that their world was collapsing, The new world order with Germany on the top was on its way out, the fact that they were even speaking to us told us that. And as far as we were concerned not before time.

There was another English speaker based in the school with whom we had had a few words, a musician who had played in a band in pre war Amsterdam. He had no optimism. The last time I saw him he was a member in a patrol that was going out and was mustering in the foyer of the school. Bomber and I were standing half way up the stairs looking down at them when our eyes met. He smiled wryly and gave a shrug of his shoulders. I wouldn't have given much for any of their chances.

We left the school during the night when some shells landed in the building and there was a fair bit of confusion. Our plan was simple: to get into the country, find a suitable spot to settle down in and hopefully the Germans would retreat over us. The first part of this plan worked fine. We got out of the town and into the country and were walking through the night when we more or less fell into a German gun pit and its sleeping crew and became prisoners yet again. Dawn came and we were dispatched to their Head Quarters in a nearby village under the guard of a member of the Volksturm, a unit of older conscripts most of whom had served in the 1914-18 war. To us at the time he seemed a very old man, probably about fifty, and he walked behind us pushing a bike with his rifle pointing our way as it rested on the saddle and the handlebars. On the carrier of his bike he had a wooden box and strapped incongruously to the top of this box there was pair of slippers. He reported to a house in the village which was the local Army H.Q.and was told to wait outside. He propped his bike and himself up against the garden wall which was about four foot high and we did the same a few yards from him. It was soon apparent that he was very tired. He kept yawning and at times nodding off. Having watched this a few times I suggested to Bomber that the next time he nodded off and closed his eyes we should swing ourselves over the wall and sit down under the bushes on the other side. We couldn't see it doing us any harm and it might do us a bit of good as obviously we were just a nuisance to the Germans and one they could so easily get rid of. It was done in second. The sentry's head drooped and when he came to we had gone. We probably moved eighteen inches. There was a bit of racing and chasing and we heard an officer screaming at the old boy but no one thought of looking over the wall under the rhododendron bushes. We stayed there all day and in early evening when they moved out we stayed put.

We heard the Russians arrive during the night but we stayed on until daylight as we did not want to be involved in any case of mistaken identity with a trigger happy Ivan. Come daylight we emerged to parrot our phrase in our fluent Russian and soon we had another rifle, another bandolier and we were back to drifting. But this time we had fellow travellers. They were all English speaking ex prisoners. It was like Noah's ark because we were all in pairs as we had all got away with our mate, cobber, buddy, oppo, partner, pal depending on whether you were an Aussie, New Zealander, American, South African, Canadian - twelve or fourteen of us in all. We were doing our normal drifting act a few days later with some of this bunch when we saw some German transport caught in a narrow road by Russian planes. It was unusual in the fact that it was motor transport, as by far the greater percentage of German transport, as it was with the Russians, was horse drawn. When one of the leading trucks was hit and set on fire it acted like a cork in a bottle in the narrow road and the whole convoy bunched up and stopped. As the planes came for a second run the Germans dived through the hedge alongside the road and into a small bit of pasture which sloped down to the wood where we were standing watching. The hedge was less than a 100 yards away - it was their unlucky day. They were out of the frying pan into the fire. A couple of them were actually running down towards the wood for shelter as we started knocking them over and we couldn't miss at such a range. We had no compunction about it as our feelings at that time was that the only good German-was a dead one. It was a bit before some of them realised what was happening and those that were at the top of the field and still able to, disappeared back through the hedge the way they had came. I think it was this day that I saw the deadest man I have ever seen. He was a Russian and when I jumped into a convenient trench quickly and gratefully when a mortar bomb came my way he was there sitting facing me. What seemed to accentuate his death was that his eyes were open but they had a fine coating of dust on them. I thought then that it was the last place in the world you expect to see dust, on somebody's eyes.

There is another mental picture I have of that time. We had entered a largish village through which the Germans had retreated and I came across half a dozen Panzerfausts in a narrow lane running off the main street. These Panzerfausts were hand held anti tank weapons and you needed to be pretty close to a tank to

do any good with them. For Germans it was an automatic, and well earned, Iron Cross if you knocked out five tanks with them. I was thinking I would like to try one out of interest - I had even chosen my target, a small brick outhouse and I was studying the weapon when for some reason I looked around and found that I was being watched impassively by a wrinkled old woman. She was small, white haired, dressed in black, and she was leaning against the door of a small neat house and was wearing a starched white apron. What makes me remember her was that the apron was completely bespattered with blood.

Shortly after our drifting came to a stop. We were outside a place called Brux which we were told was being held by the SS. Here and in other places their past was catching up with them. They had done horrific and indefensible things in Russia and it was acknowledged that the Russians did not take SS men prisoners. The Germans were quite conscious of this as I had seen prisoners who had removed their SS collar badges. But what they could not remove were the four holes in the collar itself. I also remember being told by some that they had been forced to join the SS as this would encourage them to fight harder. Knowing their probable fate the SS unit in Brux had decided to fight to the end.

By now our English speaking party had increased as other English speaking odds and sods turned up. Our latest addition made us think that there may be some truth in this fight to the death story. He was an American pilot who had been shot down. When a Russian delivered him to our billets his first words were 'What the hell are you guys doing here? The goddamn war has been over two days'"

We found a wireless set and from the gist of what was said we realised it was true, the war was over.

Our attitude changed immediately. To get the knock during the war was one thing, but when the war was over it was entirely different. If the SS and the Russians wanted to fight to the death that was up to them. But we were going home. Bomber, whom I met once after the war in 1985 and who had remembered things I had forgotten, told me we were discussing this when a large shell splinter went between us and hit the wall against which we were leaning. He said it finished the discussion and speeded our departure.

We had problems about leaving. Not that the Russians wanted to stop us but they didn't want to let us have any transport. How we got what we did I have no idea but we ended up with something ideal - a German troop transporter. We scrounged (an all embracing word) diesel and what ever else we needed and with the latest additions to our party, three Cypriots, we set off for home.

I suppose you could say they were halcyon days. We were young, alive, going home and on the winning side.

My last sight of the Russian army had English overtones. We saw a troop of Cossacks trotting into the outskirts of Brux and recognised two of them. They were Pinky and Mush who had made the unsuccessful attempt to escape by train and with whom we had been in the same Stalag. The description hard cases summed them up. They were regular soldiers, pre war gunners and as such had been taught to ride so that when they finally escaped and had landed among Cossacks they were at no disadvantage. They could ride with the best. They were obviously popular among their troop, like mascots, and one could see the reason why. On their brown Russian smocks they had rows of iron crosses. probably three or four rows of them, like scalps, which stretched from side to side of the brown smocks. To finish off their outfits they were both wearing battered but rakish top hats. They raised them to us as we left, our farewell to the Russian Army.

Germany at that time was a civilisation breaking up. It was in a state of anarchy. During the years when they had been the conquerors of Europe they had kept their country going with slave labour. Now with their once invincible armies shattered the country was full of freed slaves with scores to settle. Our attitude was good luck to them. We drove across Germany well armed, equipped and organised. What we wanted we took. It was journey of contrasts of which I can remember only too little. In one house we had commandeered for the night we were timidly woken up and asked if we would accept the surrender of about three hundred Germans who were hiding in the woods nearby. In one small town thirty six Russian prisoners died in a railway siding through drinking industrial alcohol. I was sprawled on the back of the truck with one of the Americans as it rumbled West and we passed down a narrow lane where the trees on either side were heavy with May blossom. Our passing brought these blossoms drifting down like snow flakes, the road turned white as we watched. It was amazing, an image of winter in summer. I watched enchanted. My more prosaic companion put it into words with his Southern drawl. 'Mighty purty, Mike, mighty purty.'

What more can one say?

I saw something that to me sums up the prevailing anarchy One of our party wanted to shave. The truck was parked in the main street of some small town and opposite us was a furniture store with a large ornate side board in the window. First he smashed the window of the store in. He could have gone in through the door but that did not appeal. Then he carefully knocked out sufficient glass so that he could get in through the window without cutting himself. He then broke the main mirror in the sideboard, tapped out one of the larger broken pieces until it was about the size he wanted, about four square inches, then he took it into the street where he propped it on a window sill, had his shave and walked away.

I remember being with one of the Canadians as he tried to show me how to milk a cow. Those incidents are all I can remember of a civilisation breaking up.

I cannot remember our actual meeting up with the Americans. But when I did I ended up in a hospital, as some diet deficiency had caught up with me and all my teeth were loose and on the verge of falling out. I was lucky that they were caught in time as I still have most of them today.

It was at this time Bomber and I went our different ways, he going home and me into hospital. All I remember of the hospital, and it is ingrained in my memory, was that one of the patients in the next ward was an American pilot whose plane had been shot down. His parachute had caught in the branches of a tree under which, ironically, part of his own plane was burning. He had hung there until both hands and feet had been burnt off. He pleaded not to be sent back to the States, he just wanted to die.

It seemed only a short time before I was fed back into the pipe line and sent to a transit camp from which trucks were running a shuttle service to an air field where Dakota air craft seemed to be doing the same, taking men home. The trucks were driven by out going, exuberant coloured drivers. In those days coloured men were not considered suitable for combat duties. Each truck carried fifty men standing packed like sardines, but who cared? - it was the last lap. The atmosphere in the camp was fantastic as empty trucks came roaring in and the full ones went out. It was on the narrow road to the airfield that two of them caught hubs. The empty one broke its back axle and it simply squatted down spilling oil all over the road. The other one which was only one up from ours in the convoy, rolled over upside down. It was resting on the passengers heads and they were packed so tightly they couldn't move. We had to push it over before we could get at them,then slither about on a mixture of blood, brains and oil to get them out. I remember being sick. There were nine killed. The road was cleared and shortly after we were back in England. My luck had held to the last.

I ended up in Reading where I was issued with a new battle dress, a pay book, a rail pass and told to go home and report to the nearest barracks when I needed money. This was Bury Barracks. It was the Dunkirk drill all over again. It seemed a lifetime ago since I had seen those soldiers that had got out from Dunkirk come trailing back and had then been told to report to Bury Barracks.

It was difficult to settle down and in fact I found I couldn't. I wasn't the only one. There must have been thousands of us. Jimmy Barlow, who I had last seen in a German hospital where he had treated me, was another. We took off together.

It was a marvellous time to travel in England if you wore a uniform and had a bit of ribbon on it as we had that of the African Star with an eight on it to denote we had served with the Eighth Army. The euphoria of winning the war was still there and the bit of ribbon said that we had done our bit to help win it. That bit of ribbon opened many doors, or made sure we were on the right side of them when they were being closed. Generally pubs and clubs, I must admit. We never realised how valuable it was until Jim threw his away. This happened at Edinburgh station when, as we were walking down a platform, an ATS girl came up it. She also was wearing the same bit of ribbon. Jimmy who was an impetuous sort of person and had seen a lot of the worst side of war, was incensed, ripped off his ribbon and threw it in the railway tracks. It was soon obvious that we had to get one back. Jimmy would go up to a bar for drinks and where once he would have been accepted he would get remarks such as, "Move over, soldier, and get some service in." Jimmy was lightly built but he made up for it in aggressiveness and the confidence that he knew how to handle himself. It was one fight after another until we managed to get another bit of ribbon.

England at that time was still geared up for servicemen. There were still innumerable canteens and hostels for servicemen so we had no worries about where to sleep and eat in every town. Any pub we went in we would invariably see someone who we had some sort of connection with. The eight on our ribbon alone gave us an introduction to a whole army, plus the fact that we seemed to know someone in almost every town. We looked them up and drank to old times. I often wondered why I never looked up Bomber but then I realised we never looked up any of the friends we had made who were married. Perhaps this was just commonsense. In a way we were quite snobby, or at least selective, as to who we drank with. In the army only about seven men in every hundred were at the sharp end and it only took a few minutes to find out if they had been in the seven end. It was with these we drank and, like the Abington Mashers, we didn't give a damn for tomorrow. And because of our back pay we didn't have to borrow.

This went on for weeks until there came a day when Jimmy wanted to spend all his time in Goole. Whatever town we had been in we had often ended up in dance halls and in one in Goole he had met a girl.

I returned to Radcliffe alone and I knew my mother was pleased when I dug out my walking boots and packed my sleeping bag in my rucksack. "Come to my senses" was her phrase. I had intended hitching up to the Lakes but as I went out of the door and she asked me where I was going. The Skye Boat Song was being played on the wireless so I replied Skye. I hitched up there and was fortunate in that my first visit to Skye I had fantastic weather and for a couple of weeks I scrambled about the peaks of the Cuillins at peace with the world. It was in fact what would now be called rehabilitation. Having got whatever one gets out of one's system at these times I returned home and applied for a grant to go to an art school.

Normally interrupted training was the criterion to get a Government grant and all the training the war had interrupted for me was a couple of evenings a week art classes at the local technical school. Nevertheless I put in an application and I was asked to attend a selection board at Manchester Art School. I had been before this board and was having a coffee in the canteen with two other hopeful ex service men and none of us felt very confident. Plus the fact that we felt completely out of place as the canteen was full of well spoken, well brought up middle class girls. (One of whom I later married.) During this coffee break one of the examiners drifted across to our table, coffee cup in hand and asked me 'Weren't you in the desert?' Surprised, I nodded. 'I thought I recognised you, 22nd Armoured Brigade wasn't it?" His phenomenal memory went back to me doing my Mary's little lamb act with the C.O.s map. We chatted a little of those distant days and, the coffee break over, we parted.

Whether that meeting tipped the balance I have no idea but I got my grant, was accepted for the art school and for me the war was well and truly over.

P.S. Years later my eldest daughter met and married a German whose Father had served in the Afrika Korp. we had a holiday together and he kept his citation for the Iron cross hanging in the loo!!

The war over and on honeymoon in the Bavarian Alps, not far from Hitler's retreat, the Eagle's Nest.